Military to Civilian Career

A Transition Guidebook

Angela M. Gunshore, MA

DISCLAIMER

This publication is designed to provide accurate and authoritative information regarding the subject matter covered. It is sold with the understanding that the publisher is not engaged in rendering legal, medical, or other professional services. If legal or medical advice or other expert assistance is required, the services of a competent professional person should be sought.

To request permissions, contact the publisher at angelagunshore@gmail.com

Library of Congress Cataloging-in-Publication Data

Gunshore, Angela 1974-

Military to Civilian Career: A Transition Guidebook/Angela M. Gunshore, MA

First Edition

Includes Bibliographical References

Paperback ISBN: 978-1-09838-163-9

E-book ISBN: 978-1-09838-164-6

Copyright © 2021 Angela Gunshore

www.angelagunshore.com

So many people have influenced the development of this guidebook.

First, I want to thank my Creator, who put me at the right place and the right time to meet so many amazing veterans, and for giving me the ability to be of service to them.. I also am grateful to my angels, guides, and ancestors who I believe led and supported my goals of helping others. I want to thank my family: Paul, Marianna, Gina, and Annie, for believing in me. Thank you for your patience with me during the times I was away on calls, researching, working, and writing this guidebook. I am so grateful to you.

None of this would be possible without the service members I was blessed to work with. I want to thank the veterans who allowed me to work with them in securing employment and for their trust and faith in me to help them. I also want to thank all of the career specialists, coaches and facilitators who mentored me in this career field. And I want to thank all the career advisors and program managers at the various military installations that I was privileged to meet and work with.

I dedicate this guidebook to all the service members of all branches that served in the OIF and OEF.

Wishing you all the best,

Angela

March 26, 2021

CONTENTS

Thank you for buying the Military to Civilian Career Transition Guidebook. This guidebook was created to help those who are currently in the military or have recently transitioned out of the military. The book is set up to work with you. It is set up for 12 months, but I have worked with veterans who completed the process in less than 12 weeks (less than 90 days). You can start and stop as you please. The book aims to help you clarify your goals, create a resume, prepare a cover letter, research opportunities and practice interviewing to find the best civilian career.

Inside this book are tips, sources, and worksheets that will guide you in the workforce transition. I would recommend writing in the book as you proceed through the months. Each chapter focuses on a certain topic and works together as a unified plan. The goal, as you move along the chapters in this book, is to help you prepare for the transition into a civilian career.

In each chapter, you will find a calendar in the first part. Write in this calendar and add any specific plans, goals, appointments, and actions that you wish to accomplish during the month. Remember that between work life, home life, and maybe even training or school, the time before your termination or retirement is drawing near. By setting goals each month, you will successfully prepare for the transition. Planning is essential in making the transition easier and stress-free.

You will find questions, worksheets, and activities to complete that will help you define your workforce career goals and prepare you for transition. Every branch of the military transitions differently. I have worked with all the branches in my 20 plus years and have designed this guidebook to acknowledge the differences in each branch's transition materials. Working with these materials will help define your focus over the next months.

I have also designed this book to be flexible like a manual so you can add it to your binders or carry it with you. I recommend taking this book with you when you meet with your career counselors and exit counselors. As you go through the book, it will help you define those areas of transition that will be addressed by those counselors.

This book was written to address the technology and job fields of 2021 and I suspect it will need to be revised within three years. As the DOD changes its methods to transition service members, plus the ways that companies accept resumes, the book will recommend certain sites to connect with to learn the latest methods of job recruiting. Consider bookmarking or following the recommended sites to understand the job market.

I am very excited for you to discover all the great skills and experiences you have to offer to the civilian world. This book will help you uncover all the experiences and training you have had that the civilian world needs.

Thank you again for allowing my guidebook to help you in this endeavor.

Wishing you all the best,
Angela

FIRST MONTH:

DECIDING TO TRANSITION

Create your calendar each month.

Label the Month and input the dates of the month when you will start your transition. Goal: To plan days and times to work on your transition.

Month: _____

SUNDAY	MONDAY	TUESDAY	WEDNESDAY	THURSDAY	FRIDAY	SATURDAY

The objectives for Chapter One

- To understand the decision-making process that one uses to transition from the military

- To understand the areas which the decision impacts when deciding to leave the military

- To use decision-making tools and worksheets to help the transitioning military person decide the best option for their life, family, and career.

Job Options and Market Trends

There is no wrong way to do this transition. Some of you may decide quickly that you want to leave the military. Some of you may go back and take another 10 years before you finally leave. Some of you may decide to retire but still work as a consultant or in the defense industry which technically means you are still with the military. And some of you may decide altogether to never do anything military again. Whatever your decision, this chapter is here to help you.

This chapter is devoted to helping you decide whether to stay or to go from the military. Now if you are clear in your decision to leave, you can probably skip over this chapter. But I recommend still looking at the material and maybe even doing some of the worksheets and some of the activities to see if you are ready.

I have worked with all ages of service members and all of them have different reasons for why they left the military. I have heard every reason why people want to leave the military. What this chapter is going to lay out for you are ways to make this decision. You may decide to stay. Then I would tell you to tuck this book away and revisit it at a later time. Every soldier and sailor will have to transition from the military someday and this book will help.

The Military Reason

The main reasons why people join the military usually revolve around the situation or events of the times.

In the 1980s, it was the call to serve and family histories. President Reagan had built up the military and all the popular movies were military focused. Patriotism and family ties to the military were pushed from all sectors of society. Most parents or grandparents had served at some level in the military.

1990s family history: Grampa/Gramma served WWII, Mom/Dad in Vietnam plus the incentives such as the GI Bill being the focus for why people served.

2000 was due to the situations from 9-11 to the war in Iraq. The sense of duty and call to serve.

2010 saw a rise in people wanting economic stability due to the recessions, also to help with school funding/training, adventure, and travel.

2020 saw more of the necessity for economic reasons, many also felt a call to serve, plus the benefits and travel were a major pull for some.

Why did you join the Military?
What did you expect from the Military in exchange for your service?
Did the military give you what you wanted or expected?
Regardless of why you chose to join, it was a great choice that gave you experiences like no other.

Reasons to Leave

Some reasons why people decide to leave the Military that we need to discuss:

- *Family Life* – Constant deployments, changes and moves, lack of financial raises, and the issues faced by military personnel through warfare.

- *Health and Wellness* – Constant deployments, long working hours, the environment in which you work, and of course the mental and physical stress. Continuous warfare experiences have driven up the numbers of men and women leaving the Military.

- *Rank Advancement and Leadership* – The changes in who one serves with, how groups are commanded, and who gets promoted. The desire to stay in has diminished.

- *Values Have Changed*– When the uniform is harder to put on, the purpose and passion have been lost and isolation/separation from your unit, friends, and the unit becomes the norm. It is time leave.

- *Civilian Life* – A belief that being a civilian is somehow easier and better because of fewer restrictions and rules. Also, a belief that civilian life will be more stable.

- *Temporary Solution* – A view that the military life was only temporary to gain school funding or as a stepping stone to adulthood.

- *Civilian Jobs Pay More* – A belief that you can make more money outside of the military in a civilian job doing similar work.

- ***Less Work in the Civilian World*** – Military personnel are often overworked with no overtime pay – many believe that civilian work is often paid more for less time, comparing the 8 am to 4 pm job schedule of a civilian versus that of a soldier's schedule.

- ***No Micromanagement/No Structure*** – Belief that in the civilian workplace, no one is micromanaged in the same fashion as is done in the military. Viewing the civilian workplace as lackadaisical.

This chapter is designed to work on the reasons why you should stay in the military or leave, but as you move on in this guidebook, you may decide to leave in Chapter One but stay by Chapter Five. There are more views of this decision than the ones listed above.

Let us look at the family reason. Family is everything. They will be the ones with you in your older years. They will give you the love and comfort that every human desire and needs. This decision needs to also consider their perspective. It will depend on the factors of what is important for you but also for your loved ones. I have heard many veterans tell me that they decided to retire and move back home so their families could be close to loved ones. Many told me it was only fair since they traveled for the military and now in retirement, they could choose to be near loved ones. The problem that the veterans found was that in their hometowns, there were no jobs or opportunities for them. Remember, if you have been serving for over 20 years, the hometown you left will have changed drastically and employment opportunities may have decreased. Sometimes moving hours away to a better job market is more beneficial for the family.

Health and wellness factors are sometimes out of the soldiers' control. In recent times, with COVID-19, some soldiers and sailors are considering being discharged for medical reasons as a result of becoming sick. I have worked with many medically discharged soldiers and sailors and it has always been a difficult transition due to the medical paperwork. Some would not wait for the medical discharge fearing job selection would be affected. Please consider applying for medical discharge if you can; it is worth the effort to have that medical help in the civilian world. Also, your job prospects should not be affected, many disabled veterans still qualify for multiple opportunities in the civilian world. Side note: I have had people defer their transition because of medical testing and I have seen the government defer a retirement based on needing that soldier or sailor for a mission or training. Sometimes medically discharging takes longer but the disability offerings by the VA and government are worth the wait. Seek medical information about your current conditions before making any decision to transition. You must have a VA doctor medically evaluate your conditions before exiting the military.

Let us look at when the government forces the separation. An example of this was in the 1990s when the Navy bases were being closed in certain areas across the world due to budget overhauls in the federal government. Many soldiers and sailors found themselves honorably discharged. For the first time, America saw that our military can have pink slips. It was very hard for many of the sailors and soldiers who wanted to stay till retirement, only to be told their unit or division was budget cut. Sometimes leaving is not the soldier's choice but the government's.

The military is always changing. Keep current with changes in leadership, policies, and how rank advancement occurs. Some ways that these changes can affect service. Military personnel can become frustrated with leadership especially when it effects deployment, their MOS or even the reason why they serve. Leadership in the civilian world can have these same issues. I can tell you that in the civilian world, very rarely do you get to move jobs or even locations in a company like you can in the military. Unless it is a global or manufacturing company, many American businesses hire a person to stay in that job indefinitely. The military does allow you to move your MOS, ask for a transfer and even change directions in your career. You have choices in the Military that you might not have in the civilian world.

Using the choices below, what would make you leave the military? Check all that apply:

_____ family   _____ having more freedom at a job

_____ health & wellness   _____ wanting an 8 to 4 job schedule

_____ leadership issues   _____ wanting overtime pay

_____ inability to advance in career   _____ medical discharge

_____ changes in the military   _____ tired of the deployments

_____ tired of the structure and restrictions   _____ conduct issues

_____ desire to have a "Normal" Life   _____ dislike MOS/job

_____ lack of money or opportunities   _____ other: _____

What do you love about being in the military?

The Career Decision-Making Scale

The following assessment will look at 30 different statements that cover five processes or decision steps. The goal is to see where you are in deciding the path for your career. Please read each statement and decide if it applies to you. You will choose whether to circle TRUE or FALSE based on the statement. After you are done you will add up the numbers to see your assessment in each process group.

In making career decisions....

		TRUE	FALSE
	I often let others decide things for me	1	2
	I am often unsure of decisions	1	2
	I often allow things to just happen or develop	1	2
A	I follow a specific formula to help in my decision-making	2	1
	I am a procrastinator and I wait until the last minute to decide	1	2
	I struggle to commit to a decision	1	2

Total score: _____

		TRUE	FALSE
	I take in consideration how my decision will affect others	2	1
	I do not need to research career option	1	2
	I am great at analyzing myself and it helps in making my decision	2	1
B	I consider all my skills and interests when making my decision	2	1
	I seek help from others in making my decision	2	1
	I often am overwhelmed with information	1	2

Total score: _____

		TRUE	FALSE
	I often evaluate my choices before deciding	2	1
	I seek out creative options and possibilities	2	1
	I am open to all types of career options and alternatives	2	1
C	I consider the possible outcomes before deciding	2	1
	I rationally consider all the costs and benefits of my decision	2	1
	I take time to rank and eliminate choices before deciding	2	1

Total score: _____

	TRUE	FALSE
I trust my gut/feelings over logic when deciding	2	1
I often choose the first options or possibility available to me	1	2
I am unconfident in my decision-making	1	2
D I am flexible and can compromise in my decision	2	1
I consider the fulfillment of my needs before deciding	2	1
I cannot decide even though I know I need to	1	2

Total score: _____

	TRUE	FALSE
I fear the consequences of my decisions	1	2
I am confident in taking risks in my career	1	2
I quickly act once a decision is made	2	1
E I am worried that the decision will take a lot of my time and energy	1	2
I create goals for following through on my decision	2	1
I reevaluate all choices before deciding	1	2

Total score: _____

ASSESSMENT SCORE

This assessment will help you understand your career decision-making process. For each section A, B, C, D, and E, you will add up each column based on the Number you circled under TRUE and FALSE. Record the total number for each section in the corresponding section:

A. Defining and committing to a decision _____

B. Gathering information about oneself and the overall situation _____

C. Examining and forming alternative options to the decision _____

D. Selecting the Best outcome or decision _____

E. Starting or Implementing your decision _____

What each range means:

6-7 The low numbers mean you may want to seek guidance on helping with that aspect of decision-making. It may be a good idea seek out a career coach, guidance counselor, or a talent acquisition or workplace specialist that can help define and guide you on your process for making a career decision. Pay special attention to the low-scoring sections to understand how to make the best decision for you when deciding your career. See the next section for further clarification.

8-10 Is a medium-range score and would suggest that working with a career advisor or coach would benefit but may not be needed.

11-12 is a high number which indicates that career decision-making should not pose a problem for you.

Defining Your Decision-making Process

Studies have discovered that most people do not have a career decision-making process and do not go through a step-by-step approach to figuring out the best career decision for them. The five categories that we just assessed ourselves on are based on a logical approach to developing a list of reasons, possibilities, and choices before deciding what path to take in your career transition.

A. *Defining and committing to a decision*

 1. What are your choices?

 Most people base their career options on availability and aspects that fulfill long-term goals and meet the present-day needs.

 2. What kind of employment do you need?

 Currently, many people may need remote work or no travel options in their job due to family, disability, pandemic, or illness. Some people may want a first shift job, a regular 9 to 5 position to be available for the family. And other people may want a desk job because of being on their feet in their current employment or because of disability/illness.

3. What kind of employment do you want?

This question may have requirements attached to it such as needing more education, certification, or even a license to perform job duties in a state or region. This may mean staying at the current position until requirements are met or achieved.

Pay is another aspect of this question. Some people require a certain level of salary to transition from one employment to another. Considering what type of company or position would meet the desired salary must be addressed as part of this answer.

Location of employment is another part of this question that needs to be addressed. The desired employment may not have opportunities in the current area of residence of the candidate. An example of location issues is wanting to be an aviation quality engineer or manager but living in a region with no aviation manufacturer or airfield.

B. *Gathering information about oneself and the overall situation*

1. Do I have all my employment papers, job descriptions, and certifications/degree information in one location?

Gathering all information on your education and employment experiences is crucial for preparing for your career transition. The military provides binders for all enlisted service members to maintain records of all MOS training, certifications, and rewards. Keeping this binder up-to-date is essential, especially if you are planning to transition within a year. The paperwork and record-keeping by the federal government can be backlogged and may not record up-to-date employment and training on your VMET report.

2. Education – Do I have my transcripts from all colleges that list my courses, grades, and GPA?

As you start the career transition, pay the fee to gain access to your transcripts. Print them out and save them in your binder.

3. All training – Remember all the training you experienced and acquired while serving? Is there any training before service that also can be mentioned?

All the training from First Aide to Leadership can be added to a resume and discussed in an interview. You would be surprised what civilian employers need from employees. It helps to have first responders onsite or hazmat-trained employees.

4. Security Clearance – Can I renew or add any clearances or training before I exit the military?

Security clearance is very hard to acquire in the civilian world. If your clearances are expiring soon, see if you can renew before you start the transition process. Having those clearances can make a difference in gaining employment. Same for training certification or renewal such as with OSHA, ISO, Quality, Hazmat, CPR, and First Aid, FAA, etc.

5. Spend a day shadowing a civilian job. Especially if you plan on settling in a non-familiar area. The culture shock that you experience going from military life to civilian, especially the workforce, can cause anxiety and pressure. If you plan on moving to a particular location, take your next vacation there to check the place out before submitting paperwork. Look at the local job market. See if you can visit a place of work, meet contacts, and understand what life will be like in this location or place of employment. Get your feet wet before you jump into a new lifestyle.

DECISION-MAKING WORKSHEET 1

Fill out the boxes by stating your best choices currently. And then discussing the pros and cons of each option. The goal is to find one option that is dominant from the other.

Option One:	Option Two:
Stay in the Military	Leave and Become a civilian

Pros:	Pros:
1.	1.
2.	2.
3.	3.
4.	4.

Cons:	Cons:
1.	1.
2.	2.
3.	3.
4.	4.

Results:

Based on the two options, which one looks better on paper: Opt. 1   or   Opt. 2

As you see this choice is there any hesitation on this option?   Yes   or   NO

And why do you think that is?

Decision Checklist

Decision:

What needs to be done to succeed at this decision?
1. Ex. Set up a meeting with Financial Counselor on Base
2.
3.
4.
5.
6.
7.
8.
9.

Desired Outcome from this Decision:
1. Ex. More or Equivalent Pay
2.
3.
4.
5.
6.
7.

Obstacles to reaching your goal	Solutions to overcome obstacles
Ex. Timing	Schedule time each day or week

My Decision on transition is to

_____

Confidence Meter: How Confident are you with your decision?

$$1 - 2 — 3 — 4 — 5 — 6 — 7 — 8 — 9 — 10$$

Unsure   Almost sure   Very Sure

Remember this decision is not a reality until you receive your DD-214. If you decide to wait and stay in the military, then tuck this book away until you are ready to transition. If you want to continue, head-on to Chapter 2 where we look at Finances.

SECOND MONTH:

FINANCES IN ORDER

Month: _____

SUNDAY	MONDAY	TUESDAY	WEDNESDAY	THURSDAY	FRIDAY	SATURDAY

The objectives for Chapter Two

- To understand the differences in military and civilian pay
- To understand the benefits of military versus civilian
- To lay out the finances and plan while preparing for civilian life
- To acknowledge the finances and budget needed in the civilian world.

Military pay – Allowances and Benefits

Being in the military offers financial allowances, such as tax-free pay, that you would not receive as a civilian.

Basic Pay includes: active duty, attendance at training and schools, drills, back wages

Special Pay includes hardship duty, pharmacy, aviation, and naval career duties, foreign duty, special assignment pay.

Combat Pay

Bonus Pay: Overseas extensions, reenlistment, officer, career status

Incentive Pay: Hazardous duty, HALO, and submarine

Other Pay: FSA, student loans, deployment, CONUS COLA, vehicle, life insurance, disability, education for self and children, child support, burial/funeral

Living Allowances: BAH, BAS, OHA

Moving Allowances: Paid moving trucks, storage, temporary housing, and lodging

Travel Allowances: Leave from overseas tours, transportation, and per diem

In-Kind Military Benefits: Daycare allowance, defense counsel services, medical and dental, commissary discounts, travel aboard government aircraft, supplied uniforms

Differences Between Military and Civilian Pay

1. *Gross Pay versus Net Pay*

   The gross pay or the salary you will make as a civilian is not what you will bring home. In the service, you usually receive the pay grade you expected because taxes, benefits, and retirement were not deducted from your military paycheck. The net pay will be drastically lower for civilian paychecks because your pay will see deductions for benefits.

   Military pay:
   Gross pay per week
   Minus (FICA, FITW, and SITW)

Minus (Thrift Savings Plan, Servicemembers Group Life Insurance)

Plus Combat Pay gives you the FITW and SITW back

Equals Net Pay

Civilian pay:

Gross pay per week

Minus mandatory deductions like taxes (FICA, FITW, SITW, and local)

Minus voluntary deductions like medical, life insurance, pension, and 401Ks

Equals the take-home pay or net pay.

Knowing these differences between paychecks can help one prepare for a civilian career by understanding how much salary they would need to continue their lifestyle.

There are some websites that help the military figure out the civilian salary:

https://www.dinkytown.net/java/civilian-pay-to-equal-military-take-home-pay.html

https://militarybenefits.info/military-pay-calculator/

2. *Budget with the NET pay for Home, Medical, and Food*

Take the BAH you currently receive as a guide of what you will need to budget for in working with a civilian net pay. Know your expenses by writing all your bills down including utilities, credit debt, loans, and grocery bills per month. Then using the net pay estimate the income you will need per month?

See budget examples showcased in this chapter

3. *Gather all Financial Information*

Records of your debt, loans, and your budget. Create a binder where you can log all the information for understanding your finances. Keep a monthly record of what you spend and save. Understand what you will need to live as a civilian without military allowances.

4. *Set Up a Meeting with the Personal Finance Managers (PFMs)*

They are available for you on base. It is free to talk to them and they have a wealth of information and can help financially guide you through your transition.

To contact a PFM program on your installation call 910-449-4979.

NMCRS: Navy/Marine Corps Relief Society is another organization that can work with service members to help them get out of debt, find grants, and interest-free loans. See their website at https://www.nmcrs.org/

Monthly Budget Template:

Monthly Income for (list month)

_____:

Monthly income: _____

Other income:_____

Other income:_____

Total monthly income:_____

Monthly Expenses for (list month)

_____:

Housing rent/mortgage: _____

Electric bill:_____

Gas bill:_____

Water bill:_____

Sewer/Trash bill:_____

Cable TV:_____

Internet:_____

Groceries:_____

Childcare:_____

Tuition:_____

Maintenance/Repairs:_____

Pets:_____

Insurance:_____

Credit Card 1:_____

Credit Card 2:_____

Credit Card 3:_____

Car loan 1:_____

Car loan 2:_____

Gas for Car:_____

Gifts/Charity:_____

Religious tithes:_____

Savings:_____

Other:_____

Medical:_____

Total amount of monthly expenses:

_____

Cash Flow for the month:

Total of monthly income:_____

Subtract (-)

Total amount of monthly expenses: _____

Equals (=)

Cash Flow for the month: _____

Based on your current answer for cash flow from the worksheet on the previous page, do you now see where you may need to prepare a budget for transitioning....The next section will help you prepare for civilian monthly bills

Financial Preparations for a Transition from a Military to a Civilian Life

The following financial preparations for a military transition to civilian life are not mandatory but offered as a way to comfortably transition.

1. Begin saving money. I would recommend at least nine months of living expenses saved before exiting the military. Let me explain why: the military benefits and offerings allow active-duty personnel to enjoy living, medical, and even food allowances that will be gone after the transition is complete. Civilian paychecks are not the same as the military. The paychecks will have taxes, medical, and other items taken out that are not normally taken from military pay. Learning to live with less while transitioning will help until a civilian position and a financial system is in place for your new civilian life.

2. Look into your Servicemembers Civil Relief Act (SRCA) benefits to see if any interest payments or loan interest deductions can be returned to you or lowered for you while being an active-duty military personnel.

   See the legal information on this Act at https://www.justice.gov/servicemembers/servicemembers-civil-relief-act-scra and see the DOD's information on this Act at https://scra.dmdc.osd.mil/scra/#/home

   Here is information from a few different banks, credit card companies, and organizations that are bound by SCRA:

   American Express: https://www.americanexpress.com/us/help-support/service-members-civil-relief/

   Bank of America: https://www.bankofamerica.com/military-banking/military-banking-faqs/

   Capital One: https://www.capitalone.com/military/faqs

   Apply in person or through their website by filling out their SCRA form

   Chase: https://www.chase.com/digital/military/scra or Call Chase Military Services at 1-877-469-0110

   Citigroup: has a division of military specialists to discuss SCRA benefits by calling 877-804-1082 in the U.S. and 605-335-2222 for overseas, they are available 24/7.

   Discover: https://www.discover.com/credit-cards/member-benefits/scra-benefits/

   Synchrony Bank: Call 1-800-232-6954: provide social security number and a recent LES.

   USAA: https://www.usaa.com/inet/wc/bank-military-scra-benefits

   Wells Fargo: https://www.wellsfargo.com/military/scra-commitments/
   Contact Wells Fargo Credit Card services at 1-800-642-4720

If any of the banks or companies show issues with your active-duty status, make sure you meet with your installation PFM and seek advice from legal assistance on your rights with SCRA.

Make sure you read about SCRA before accessing the legal office at https://legalassistance.law. af.mil/

3. Life, home, and auto insurance—start looking for insurances that could bundle all three for you before you exit the military. Remember the Servicemember's Group Life Insurance (SGLI) policy expires shortly after you leave the service. Some convert their SCLI to a Veteran Group's Life insurance which will have no medical underwriting required if you apply before your termination date. VA.gov offers a life insurance calculator to help you determine how much life insurance you would need at https://insurance.va.gov/ NeedsCalculator.

4. Survivor Benefit Plan (SBP) is another program that you will need to complete before you retire from the military. This plan needs to be set before you retire. Changes can be made after retirements such as adding a new spouse or child. The goal was to help spouses who survive their military spouses by allowing 6.5% of the Military retirement coverage to be held for the surviving spouse. You lower this percentage before you retire. If you are divorced, then you still need to contact the Defense Finance Accounting Service (DFAS) to let them know of your situation and in some cases, the spouse coverage can be converted to former spousal coverage. This plan also helps children of military veterans. Children are eligible for SBP payments if under 18 or while in school under 22. Children can be given coverage without spouse coverage but if you are married and you do not want to cover your spouse, you will need to get a written agreement from your spouse. IF you are not married but have children, then the Children Only category would need to be selected.

5. Thrift Savings Plan must be dealt with before retiring or transition. You can decide to leave the TSP account with the present funds in it. You can roll your funds into an IRA account or you can roll the funds into your new employer's retirement plan. All the choices are tax-free. Here is a list of Retirement Plans available https://www.irs.gov/retirement-plans/plan-sponsor/types-of-retirement-plans

6. Military Spouses Residency Relief Act has been a blessing on taxes for the military who live in states that deduct a state tax. Once transition occurs, those taxes will be required. Also knowing if your state takes out state taxes will help you prepare for your transition. Estimating what percentage of taxes will be deducted from your weekly pay can help you gauge where money will be missing once a civilian. Also, research how your state treats pensions for tax, especially if you will receive military retirement pay.

7. OCONUS and Earned Income Credit on your civilian taxes. See the IRS website on the taxes that will change once active-duty ends: https://www.irs.gov/publications/p3#en_US_2015_publink1000176279

8. Taxes and pay issues based on location after the military termination needs to be investigated before leaving the service. The impact of local, state, and federal taxes taken from your paycheck means the civilian

take-home pay will be drastically different than the current military take-home pay. Plan on this should read incoming pay, budget for it, and determine how it will impact your living situation.

9. Retirement pay warning. Retirees, remember your retirement pay does not begin instantly. Plan on a delay of at least two months before receiving your first payment. Some states do not tax military retirement pay, and some states do. Check to see if your state of civilian residence does deduct taxes from your retirement pay.

10. Unemployment Compensation for Ex-service members (UCX) is for honorably discharged, active-duty US military personnel. Remember to file for unemployment which is granted for six months after leaving the military. I have heard some people say that they are too proud to consciously take this unemployment and my advice is that you earned it from all those late nights, double shifts, and no overtime pay. So, apply for it through your state workforce agency. But to receive it, you need to apply for it. Also, do not wait for this check, have money saved for the first three to six months of bills to transition easier. See https://oui.doleta.gov/unemploy/ucx.asp to learn more about this compensation for ex-servicemembers.

How to Keep a Budget for Transition

1. Create a binder in which to keep all your bills, statements, receipts, and budget worksheet.

2. Set a day once a week to review your binder, pay your bills, and understand your spending.

3. Set up automatic payments if possible, to ease the burden of added fees or lost bills.

4. Cancel subscriptions and unnecessary expenses until your budget allows for savings…think about canceling items such as:

    Gyms and fitness centers – work out on base or at home
    Magazines, video memberships, and organization fees
    Stop eating at restaurants or purchasing convenience items such as coffee to go.
    Recreational activities and social spending.

5. Set a goal of an amount you want to save and track each week how close you are getting to achieving that financial goal.

6. Set up a savings fund or automatic savings deduction from your checking each week or month to help you save. View this deduction like a bill that is required each month.

7. Get everyone in the family on board with this plan. Make the goals about the family to help ease the transition and allow the other family members to feel connected.

Examples of a Budget worksheet:

Month/Year:_____

Bill	Total Amount Owed	Monthly Amount Owed	Due Date	Paid Date	Method	Amount Paid
Ex. Mortgage	$195,465.34	$1,650.88	12/1	11/20	Ck# 1232	$1,650.88
Mortgage/Rent						
Gas						
Electric						
Sewer/Trash						
Water						
HOA						.
Car Payment						
Cable						
Internet						
Cell Phone						
Credit Card 1						
Credit Card 2						
Life insurance						
Medical bill						.
Childcare						
Groceries						
Car fuel						
School Loan						
Pharmacy						
Fitness Membership						
Added to Savings Acct						

Total Expenses for the month :_____ Monthly Income:_____

Cash Flow for the month:_____

Now that you have looked at your finances and have met with your PFM on base, it is time to check in with yourself about transitioning.

My Decision on transition is to

_____

Confidence Meter: How Confident are you with your decision?

$$1 - 2—3—4—5—6—7—8—9—10$$

Unsure   Almost sure   Very Sure

Remember this decision is not a reality until you receive your DD-214. If you decide to wait and stay in the military, then tuck this book away until you are ready to transition. If you want to continue, head-on to the next chapter

THIRD MONTH:

MEDICAL INSURANCE AND BENEFITS

Month: _____

SUNDAY	MONDAY	TUESDAY	WEDNESDAY	THURSDAY	FRIDAY	SATURDAY

The objectives for Chapter Three

- To understand the medical benefits for transitioning Military personnel
- To understand the medical and insurance decisions for civilian life
- Explained pathways for medical and insurance after separating from the military

Medical Benefits for Active-Duty

Tricare Prime is the major medical insurance for active-duty personnel. Families of soldiers and sailors can choose between Tricare Prime and Tricare Select. Also, for those serving overseas, Tricare Prime has an overseas option that covers servicemembers and family.

Tricare offers to provide an assigned care manager (PCM) who will assist the Military personnel or their family with coordinating care, maintaining health records and appointments, and referring patients to a specialist in the area. Almost always, the care is provided in a Military hospital or clinic on base. Tricare Prime Members should always seek advice from their PCM before going to a civilian doctor or specialist to make sure the care is covered.

To access the Tricare site, use the https://milconnect.dmdc.osd.mil/milconnect website.

Medical Benefits for Separating Transitioning Servicemembers

Tricare offers a Transition Assistance Management Program (TAMP) that offers transitional Tricare coverage to separating active-duty military personnel and their family. But **the Tricare coverage is only for six months from the date of separation.** And you must be eligible based on four categories to receive these six months of Tricare coverage:

A. Involuntarily separated from active-duty and their eligible family members

B. National Guard or Reserves who separated from active-duty after being called up in support of a contingency operation for an active period of 30 days.

C. Separated from active-duty after being involuntarily retained in support of a contingency operation

D. Separated from active-duty following a voluntary agreement to stay active-duty for less than one year in support of a contingency mission.

Transitioning Active-Duty military and their families need to enroll in the Tricare Prime TAMP offer before the servicemember terminates their active-duty.

Transitioning Requirements for Medical release

Transitioning servicemembers will go through a Separation History and Physical Examination (SHPE) or what the VA calls a "Disability Exam" to see if any service-related injuries have occurred while serving. Check out the website: https://www.health.mil/Military-Health-Topics/Access-Cost-Quality-and-Safety/Access-to-Healthcare/DoD-VA-Sharing-Initiatives/Separation-Health-Assessment

The SHPE will assess and record:

- Medical history

- Current health condition

- Medical concerns that were identified or known during the military service

- Steps to meet this requirement:

1. Schedule your exam at the military hospital, clinic, or facility at least 180 days before you separate.

    - If you are filing a VA claim you will have to schedule it no later than 90 days before your last day

    - For extended terminal leave, schedule with a VA hospital or clinic.

    - If deployed or overseas, follow the Services' guidance for scheduling.

    - To find a VA hospital near you: https://www.va.gov/directory/guide/division.asp?dnum=3

2. DD 2807-1 needs to be filled out and completed before the exam: https://www.esd.whs.mil/Portals/54/Documents/DD/forms/dd/dd2807-1.pdf

3. The physician will review your form and address all claims in the exam report to become part of your official record.

4. The physician will review all medical history, the DD form 2807-1, and your current health assessment to see if further treatment or evaluations need to be addressed before separating.

5. DOD and VA have access to your results. You will be able to access your results through the TOL Patient Portal at www.tricareonline.com

    - If you file a VA claim you will not need to have another exam and you can file claims years after leaving the service.

    - To find information on how to file a VA disability claim go to https://www.ebenefits.va.gov/ebenefits/homepage

Medical Benefits for Retiring Servicemembers

***Before I begin this section I want to remind you that if a military website does not end in **.mil** and if a US Federal government website does not end in **.gov**, please be aware that the address could be from a fraudulent websites trying to phish for your personal information.

Always research the website, the business, and the entity before giving any of your information.

As a military retiree, you have several programs you will be eligible for. You will need to research each program and discuss with your benefits coordinator what will work best for you and your health.

Here are the current programs that you may be eligible to participate in:

1. VA Disability Compensation: If a disability has been discovered you could receive monthly compensations.

   - A veteran could be compensated for:

   - Injury in the line of service.

   - An injury that causes unemployability

   - A disabled spouse

   - For children, spouse or dependent parent (s)

   Apply online for the fastest results once you know what your disability is at https://www.va.gov/disability/how-to-file-claim/

   Also, know that the VA and DOD have a joint Pre-DISCHARGE program that helps veterans file disability compensation up to 180 days before separating or retiring from active-duty. If the transitioning service member used the program, they can expect a decision on their claim before separating.

   For more information on the Pre-Discharge benefits program, Tricare Health Plans, and other Benefits see https://www.ebenefits.va.gov/ebenefits/featured

2. VA Medical Benefits: By law, VA Hospitals are to provide as-needed care and services to promote, preserve, and restore the health of the veteran. The "needed" will be up to the healthcare provider and following accepted standards of clinical practice. VA uses priority groups to the provide care management to assure that each veteran receives services.

   Some health programs that the VA offers: https://www.publichealth.va.gov/exposures/health-concerns.asp

   - PTSD treatment – https://www.ptsd.va.gov/

   - Traumatic Brain Injury - https://www.ptsd.va.gov/professional/treat/cooccurring/tbi_ptsd_vets.asp

   - Blindness Rehabilitation - https://www.rehab.va.gov/PROSTHETICS/blindrehab/locations.asp

- Agent Orange Exposure - https://www.va.gov/disability/eligibility/hazardous-materials-exposure/agent-orange/

- Gulf War Syndrome and illnesses SW Asia- https://www.va.gov/disability/eligibility/hazardous-materials-exposure/gulf-war-illness-southwest-asia/

- Gulf War Illnesses Afghanistan - https://www.va.gov/disability/eligibility/hazardous-materials-exposure/gulf-war-illness-afghanistan/

- Radiation Exposure - https://www.va.gov/disability/eligibility/hazardous-materials-exposure/ionizing-radiation/

- Asbestos - https://www.va.gov/disability/eligibility/hazardous-materials-exposure/asbestos/

- Water Contamination - https://www.va.gov/disability/eligibility/hazardous-materials-exposure/camp-lejeune-water-contamination/

- HIV/AIDS treatment - https://www.hiv.va.gov/index.asp

- Project 112 or Project Shad- https://www.va.gov/disability/eligibility/hazardous-materials-exposure/project-112-shad/

- Mustard Gas or lewisite - https://www.va.gov/disability/eligibility/hazardous-materials-exposure/mustard-gas-lewisite/

- Substance Abuse and Mental Health Services: https://www.samhsa.gov/

3. VA Home Loan: The Department of Veterans Affairs Home Mortgage loan is for qualified veterans to help them build, buy or refinance a home with as little as $0 down, great interest rates, no mandatory cap of the financial amount, and no Private Mortgage Insurance (PMI). For more information go to https://www.va.gov/housing-assistance/#get-va-home-loan-benefits

The VA also has Disability Veterans Housing Grants that help disabled veterans make changes to their homes to live more independently.

To be eligible for this Specially Adapted Housing Grant:

You must:

- Own or will own your home

- Have a qualifying service-connected disability

For more information on qualifications and how to apply: https://www.va.gov/housing-assistance/disability-housing-grants/

4. Readjustment Counseling: Vet Centers across the USA provide individual, family, and group counseling to help make the transition to civilian successful. PTSD treatment and other military-related problems can be treated to help the veteran cope with family, work, school, and everyday life. The Vet Center also provides

other psycho-social services including medical referrals, outreach, and homeless Veterans services. See www.vetcenter.va.gov/ or call 877-WAR-VETS (877-927-8387) for more information.

Eligibility for the Vet Center depends on if the veteran or active-duty servicemember

- Served in the combat theater
- Experienced military sexual trauma
- Worked or provided medical care or mortuary services
- Served with unmanned aerial vehicle crew that supported combat operations
- Is a Vietnam-era veteran who received care before 2013

Also, family members of veterans are eligible if the issue is military-related or they need bereavement counseling. Vet Center bereavement services can be accessed at 202-461-6530.

5. Education and Career Counseling: The VA offers personalized individual career counseling for active-duty service members, veterans, and their dependents to help with career guidance, effective use of the VA benefits, and resources to fulfill their goals.

   Eligibility for VA Education and Career Counseling:

   - Active-Duty service member that is six months from transitioning or discharge
   - A veteran within one year from separating from service
   - Any service member eligible for the GI Bill
   - Anyone receiving the GI Bill

   To apply for this free career counseling, you must complete the VA Form 28-8832 (https://www.vba.va.gov/ pubs/forms/VBA-28-8832-ARE.pdf) and mail it to the nearest VA Regional Office – Attention: Vocational Rehabilitation and Employment. Once accepted you will be asked to attend an orientation session at the nearest VA regional facility.

6. Burial benefits: This information should be provided for your family members and kept with your life insurance information, your end-of-life plan, and your DD-214. The VA provides cash allowances to eligible veteran families to help cover the cost of the burial and funeral of the veteran. The amount depends on if the death was service-connected or if the veteran was hospitalized with the VA at the time of death. If the veteran does not have a next of kin, the VA will also furnish the casket or urn for interment in a veteran cemetery.

   To be eligible for this service:

   - The veteran had to die as a result of a service-connected disability
   - Was receiving VA pension or compensation at the time of death

- Was entitled to VA pension or compensation but received military retirement or disability

- Died in a VA hospital while receiving care

- Died in a VA-approved state nursing home

For the family to receive this benefit they would need to fill out VA Form 21P-530 (https://www.vba.va.gov/pubs/forms/VBA-21P-530-ARE.pdf) with a copy of the DD-214 and death certificate.

Other Burial Benefits

(in most cases a funeral director would know of these benefits but just in case here they are)

1. The VA also furnishes government headstones or markers for no charge for any veteran in any cemetery around the world regardless of the date of demise. Family members must fill out VA Form 40-1330 (https://www.vba.va.gov/pubs/forms/VBA-21P-530-ARE.pdf) for marker

2. The VA also furnishes medallions for graves regardless of private or VA-supplied headstones. Family members would need to fill out VA Form 40-1330M (https://www.va.gov/vaforms/va/pdf/VA40-1330M.pdf)

3. Burial flags are also furnished at no fee to drape over the casket or accompany the urn. Family members would need VA Form 27-2008 (https://www.va.gov/vaforms/va/pdf/VA40-1330M.pdf).

4. Presidential Memorial Certificate is issued to the family of an honorably discharged deceased veteran bearing the signature of the current President. Family members would need to fill out VA Form 40-0247 (https://www.va.gov/vaforms/va/pdf/VA40-0247.pdf) to apply for this certificate. The form needs to be faxed with supporting documents to the local VA office.

5. Cemetery internment:

   a. Arlington National Cemetery: honorably discharged veterans are eligible to be buried here based on the following criteria:

      - Died on active-duty

      - Retired from the Military

      - Received a Purple Heart or Silver Star

      - A POW who died after 1993.

      The family can contact 877-907-8585 to apply for this cemetery interment and copies of the veteran's DD-214 plus death certificate will be needed when calling.

   b. Veteran Cemetery: Veterans can now find out their eligibility for burial in a VA National Cemetery before the time of need. The VA Pre-need determination form is VA FORM 40-10007 (https://www.va.gov/vaforms/va/pdf/VA40-10007.pdf) The VA then can assign gravesites to those who qualify to reserve that space. The family can call 800-535-1117 to request burial.

c. Burial at Sea by a US Military Vessel is limited to

- Active-duty servicemembers

- Retired and veterans who were honorably discharged

- Dependents of active-duty service members, retirees, and veterans

- The family would contact the Navy and Marine Mortuary Affairs Office at 866-787-0081.

Benefit Transition Workshop

During your mandatory Transition Assistance Program (TAP) you will be provided a workshop on VA Benefits. The workshop will explain the VA benefits, services and resources to help you successfully transition to your civilian life. This workshop would be a great place to ask any questions on the benefits provided by the Veterans Administration.

Veterans.gov is a great site that offers direct links for TAP and provides information on VA Benefits

The following workbook is provided during TAP, take some time to look it over before going to this workshop: https://www.benefits.va.gov/TRANSITION/docs/VA-Benefits-Participant-Guide.pdf#

My Decision on transition is to

_____

Confidence Meter: How Confident are you with your decision?

1 – 2—3—4—5—6—7—8—9—10

Unsure   Almost sure   Very Sure

Remember this decision is not a reality until you receive your DD-214. If you decide to wait and stay in the military, then tuck this book away until you are ready to transition. If you want to continue, head-on to the next chapter

FOURTH MONTH:
GOVERNMENT CLASSES AND TRAININGS

Month: _____

SUNDAY	MONDAY	TUESDAY	WEDNESDAY	THURSDAY	FRIDAY	SATURDAY

The objectives for Chapter Four:

- To understand the workshops and avenues for servicemembers to complete in transition from the military

- To learn about opportunities for training and educational degrees while active

- To understand the college and training options and accreditation.

Required Programs for Military Transition

The Transition Assistance Program (TAP) is a three to a five-day workshop designed by the Department of Labor, VA, Department of Education, Homeland Security, Small Business Administration, and the DOD to help active-duty service members move successfully into civilian sectors.

The program can be taken within the first few months of deciding to transition but should be taken before there is 90-days left of separating.

To schedule your TAP workshop, go to https://tapevents.org/

Some advice on where to take your TAP course. If you know where you want to move to or live after separating from the military, then try taking that TAP workshop in that location. Sometimes the base near where you want to live will have information or knowledge on employment in that location and it helps to receive benefits or resources. For example, if you live in Japan for active-duty but you want to live in Texas after separating, schedule to take your TAP workshop in Texas (multiple installations to choose from).

Also remember you can take your classes at joint bases such as Naval Air Stations but if you take the class in a non-joint base and you are not of that branch, the workshop will be geared towards that specific branch. So, if you are Navy or Marine, I would recommend sticking with your branch workshops because the Army workshops are geared for their MOS job classifications, their training, and their jobs. What the Army labels a MOS is different than what Marines label the same type of job.

Before you take your TAP workshop you will need to schedule an appointment with the TAP counselor for pre-separation counseling. With the TAP counselor, you will complete a self-assessment and develop an Individual Transition Plan (ITP). This must be done no later than 365 days before transition. The TAP counselor is a great resource to help you understand benefits, requirements, and entitlements. Spouses and caregivers can also attend counseling and TAP workshops.

Virtual TAP workshops do exist, especially during the COVID-19 pandemic and deployment situations. If you decide to complete all of your TAP required workshops online go to https://tapevents.org/courses

Before deciding how to fulfill this requirement (location or format) talk to your peers who have already experienced this workshop, find out what they learned, how it benefited them to attend in-person or completely online, and see what type of workshop is best for you. When I taught the TAP workshop, I added information about the local Texas and Oklahoma job markets, and I stayed during lunch and session breaks to help the service members with questions or with their resume. My workshops were based at a smaller NAS installation, but word spread, and soon I had service members from Japan, San Diego, Jackson, and the UK attend in-person to get the extra help.

Not every instructor is the same because of background and based on who runs the contract, but most are retired veterans who have experienced the transition and want to help. So do your research and go with questions, all your materials, and be excited about this new adventure.

Other Training and Programs to Consider Taking Before Transitioning

While you are on active-duty, there are so many free or reduced training that will help you gain an employment edge in the civilian workforce. But I want to caution you about what to look for and give you some criteria to look for when deciding upon a school. Unfortunately, many unaccredited schools will gladly bill your GI Bill allowances but leave you with a faulty certification or degree. Do your research and be informed before you commit to a program.

Some criteria to look for:

1. *School website address*: Most legitimate and accredited schools' website address will end in **.edu**. If the school does not end in **.edu**, then research the school, check state and federal sites for accreditation and search for any issues with their certification or degree.

2. *Know the difference between a certification and a certificate*. Anyone can give a certificate, but certification requires education, training, and testing before it can be given. Employers want certifications. Some schools will offer a certificate, so make sure what you are paying for or signing up for is what you need.

3. *Research the trade school and the job placement of their graduates*. Also, research who hires them. Some businesses will stay away from certain schools because their training is inferior, their students are not prepared, or their handling of co-ops and internships is not legit. Research and find out if the schools are worth the time or money. I often recommend seeking out community colleges as they offer the same certifications at a fraction of the cost and with the ability to earn college-level credits that can be transferred to a degree later. And many employers prefer a **.edu** school, such as a community college, over a trade school setting for their employees because many offer incentives to continue with educational opportunities and grow their employee's expertise.

4. *Yellow Ribbon Programs* is a college program that helps military and veterans receive financial help beyond the GI Bill to pay for private, state, and graduate school tuition, books, and supplies. It is up to the private and public colleges and universities to participate in this program to help service members with obtaining a degree. If you are attending school or thinking about it, look at the schools in this program. Sometimes going to a private school offers more funding than public institutions. To find out if your school participates in the Yellow Ribbon Program go to https://www.va.gov/education/yellow-ribbon-participating-schools/

5. *Seek out the Veteran-friendly programs and Veteran Services offices at educational institutions before applying*. Most colleges, trade schools, and universities have a Veteran Office on campus. See Student Veterans of America to understand if your chosen college offers a veteran office or services at www.student-veterans.org. Some refer to it as the Office of Veteran Services or Veteran Affairs. This office has trained advisors who are ready to help any veteran or military student with college admission, understanding your

military credits and certification and how to find if any of those American Council of Education Credits on your VMET or your Joint Services Transcript (JST) will transfer to your degree program. ***Always check your JST to make sure it is up to current date before transitioning out of the service and sending to any college.*** It is very difficult and time consuming to fix this JST after you separate.

6. ***Many universities that are Military-focused will allow transfer of up to 90 credits including credits for Military certifications.*** I strongly suggest that you research, locate, and call the Veteran Services office of that school before applying. Ask questions about their availability to help military students. Seek out support groups and programs to help you manage the school requirements and to cope with the civilian transition. And find out what the school has to offer you in the way of academics, counseling, and funding to help you be successful in your education. Military-friendly colleges have professors trained to work with active-duty and veteran students. At Military-focused colleges, the classes are usually filled with active-duty and veteran students. Sometimes this setting can help with the adjustment to becoming a student and a veteran. Also, some military-focused colleges and universities have extension options per class to help active-duty or reserve military students successfully pass the course despite needing field or deployment time away from the classroom. Remember to consider this if applying to colleges while still serving.

7. ***Take advantage of the Military Certifications offered on the job and on the base.*** Before exiting the military, renew: Security Clearances, First Aid and Triage/CPR, OSHA and Hazmat Certifications, Project Management, Quality Control, Scrum or Agile, FAA certifications such as the AT-CTI (Air Traffic Collegiate Training Initiative) or the A&P mechanic certificates. The Military equivalent can be transferred to the civilian FAA certification before transitioning.

Veterans' Educational Assistance Program (VEAP)

The $2 to $1 government-match program for educational assistance for those who are serving in our nation's military. To be eligible for this assistance:

- Served for the first time between 1/1/1977 and 6/20/1985 for all branches of the military except the Air Force.

- For Air Force: Served for the first time between 12/1/1980 and 9/30/1981 and enlisted in these Air Force Specialists 20723, 20731, 20830, 46130, 46230 A, B, C, D, E, F, G, H. J. or Z, 46430, 81130 and enlisted in one of the following locations Buffalo, NY; Dallas, TX; Fargo, ND; Houston, TX; Jackson, MS; Beckley, WV; Omaha, NB; Memphis, TN; Louisville, KY; Seattle, WA; Sioux Falls, SD; Syracuse, NY.

- Opened a VEAP account and deposited money into before 4/1/1987

- Put at least $25 of your own money into this account

- Finished your first period of service and did not receive a dishonorable discharge.

Apply for this assistance program at https://www.va.gov/education/other-va-education-benefits/veteran-rapid-retraining-assistance/apply-for-vrrap-form-22-1990s/introduction

Edith Nourse Rogers Stem Scholarship

Eligible Veterans and dependents in high demand fields can extend their Post-9/11 Bill or Fry Scholarship benefits. To be eligible

- Currently enrolled in an undergraduate STEM degree program OR

- Earned a post-secondary degree or graduate degree in approved STEM degree field and enrolled in clinical training program for health professionals OR

- Earned a post-secondary degree approved STEM degree field and working toward a teaching certification.

See more about this scholarship and approved STEM degree fields at https://www.va.gov/education/other-va-education-benefits/stem-scholarship/

Apply for this scholarship at https://www.va.gov/education/other-va-education-benefits/stem-scholarship/apply-for-scholarship-form-22-10203/introduction

Where to Find Certification Courses While Serving

1. ***Defense Activity for Non-Traditional Education Support (DANTES)*** go to https://www.dantes.doded.mil/

2. ***College Opportunities Online Locator (COOL)*** Check out your branch's COOL website. For your convenience, many COOL websites are now offered as apps for your phones.

   - US Army COOL: https://www.cool.osd.mil/army/

   - US Navy COOL: https://www.cool.navy.mil/

   - US Marine COOL: https://www.cool.navy.mil/usmc/index.htm

   - US Air Force COOL: https://afvec.us.af.mil/afvec/af-cool/welcome

   - US Coast Guard COOL: https://www.cool.osd.mil/uscg/index.htm

   - US National Guard COOL: https://www.nationalguard.com/education-programs/credentialing-assistance

3. The US Army is now offering a ***Credentialing Assistance (CA) programs*** that is replacing GoArmEd and this group can help you advance your career at armyignited.com. You can submit your training or exam 30 days before starting to get this processed for rank advancement or pay.

   The US Marine Corps just suspended the 6-months remaining in service requirement for funding and service members can now receive funding up to 60 days before separating.

   The US Air Force also offers a separate website to help with schooling and training that connects their COOL at https://afvec.us.af.mil/afvec/public/welcome

4. Seek out all avenues of funding before using the ***GI Bill.*** Some state schools offer veterans free or reduced tuition, assistance with living, medical, and supplies for school. Some businesses offer apprenticeships that pay for housing, books, school/training, and supplies. Scholarships are plentiful for veterans and military

students. Seek out information on ways to pay for school before signing over the GI Bill or any military funding. Also learn about the GI Bill benefits in each school: https://www.va.gov/education/choosing-a-school/

5. *Apprenticeships* can be used before transitioning if you qualify for the **DOD SkillBridge** program. A DOD SkillBridge program works with apprenticeships to place active-duty before separation in companies. The service member must find their apprenticeship before applying to the SkillBridge program. The next section in this chapter will go into detail about the DOD SkillBridge program. Also remember, an apprenticeship application, program, or schooling should not cost you a dime and the program should pay you an hourly wage plus supplies while training for the job position. Watch out for websites and companies asking for payment or to pay a fee to link you to an apprenticeship. Most legit companies have an application process on their business website. If you do not see one but know of the program, then call the business's Career Office or Human Resource Division for more information. You should never have to go through a second or third party or pay a fee to apply for an apprenticeship.

A great site for veterans to find apprenticeships: https://www.apprenticeship.gov/career-seekers/service-members-and-veterans

Examples of Companies that offer Apprenticeships

Cummins: https://cummins-apprenticeship.jobs/ (Global opportunities and they are a Defense Contractor)

General Electric has multiple apprenticeships https://jobs.gecareers.com/power/global/en/job/GE11GLOBALR3539934EXTERNALENGLOBAL/Machinist-Apprentice-Program

https://www.gehealthcare.com/about/apprentice-job

https://jobs.gecareers.com/global/en/students

Lockheed Martin: https://www.lockheedmartinjobs.com/apprenticeships

IAM/Boeing: https://www.iam-boeing-apprenticeship.com/

Roto-Rooter: https://www.rotorooter.com/careers/plumbing-apprenticeships/

Northrop Grumman https://www.northropgrumman.com/jobs/

Examples of Labor Unions that Offer Apprenticeships

IEC Fort Worth: https://www.iecfwtc.org/electrical-apprenticeship/

IEC National Chapter: https://www.ieci.org/apprenticeship

IBEW: https://electricianapprenticehq.com/how-to-join-ibew-apprenticeship/

UA Plumbers, Fitters, Welders & Service Techs: http://www.ua.org/apprenticeship

Iron Workers: http://www.ironworkers263.org/apprenticeship.html

Examples of State Apprenticeships

Hawaii: http://labor.hawaii.gov/wdd/home/job-seekers/apprenticeship/

New York: https://www.labor.ny.gov/apprenticeship/appindex.shtm

Ohio: https://apprentice.ohio.gov/index.stm

Texas: https://www.tdlr.texas.gov/electricians/apply/businesses/apprentice-programs.htm

6. ***Co-ops, Practicums, and Internships*** Most universities will allow service members to complete their co-op or internship on base and within their MOS. But if you are going for a career outside your current MOS, you can apply for the DOD SkillBridge program if you are within a year to six months of separating and you have approval by your Commanding Officer (CO) to transfer from your current MOS to this SkillBridge appointment.

Another way to complete the Co-op or Internship is to work on weekends (if you have it off) or take a leave for one to two weeks to get some experience. The majority of military students will use their current MOS for their work experience co-op or wait until they separate to gain a practicum or internship. Most co-ops are paid positions that last from four weeks to a year depending on the major and college. Internships can be paid or unpaid depending on the field. Most government internships are non-paid, but some non-profits internships are paid.

Practicums are used in teaching, counseling, medical, and research science career fields. The practicums usually last from six weeks to six months and depending on the requirements, they count as college credit which you pay for and they are not paid. It is required to get licensed in the major field to have done a practicum. The amount depends on the state requirement for licensure on how many practicums and how many hours are needed to meet the criteria.

7. ***Volunteering*** can also get you experience and can be done on your own time. If you are going for accounting and need experience, volunteer to help a non-profit or a school PTA's budgeting and accounting. If you are going for welding or machine repair, volunteer to help a non-profit, habitat organization, or community center with their maintenance. If you want to work as a social worker, teacher, or minister, volunteer with youth groups, detention centers, and shelters. Volunteering does equal training and experience that can be added to your resume in the civilian sector.

8. ***Veteran Rapid Retraining Assistance Program (VRRAP)*** VRRAP offers education and training for veterans effected by COVID and unemployment. To apply for this program go to https://www.va.gov/education/other-va-education-benefits/veteran-rapid-retraining-assistance/apply-for-vrrap-form-22-1990s/introduction

   - To be eligible for this opportunity you need to be:
   - 22 to 60 years of age
   - Unemployed because of COVID-19 pandemic

- Not eligible for GI Bill or VR& E Benefits

- Not rated as totally disbabled

- Not enrolled in a federal or state job program

- Not receiving unemployment benefits

This training program is for high-demand jobs and includes associate degrees, certificates and non-college programs. Here is a list of those 2021 High Demand occupations: https://benefits.va.gov/GIBILL/docs/vrrap-high-demand-occupation-list.pdf

Certifications for Civilian Careers

Here are some current training that can be done in the military using current MOS positions that have big advantages to gaining civilian jobs.

1. *Project Management Professional Certification (PMP)*

   PMP Certification is considered a globally recognized training that showcases to employers that you are not only capable of managing projects but have been recognized through training and examination to possess top skills in leadership. In 2021, the PMP exam and training were overhauled to create a new focus on people and business leadership. The Military branches encourage their leaders to participate and obtain this certification.

   Syracuse University's Institute for Veteran & Military families, through their Onward to Opportunity (O2O) training division, offers **free** PMP certifications for active-duty members. Also, programs for veterans to receive this PMP certification and some military installations offer their training in-person. https://ivmf.syracuse.edu/programs/career-training/learning-pathways/

   PMP criteria:

   - A four-year degree (in any subject)

   - 36 months leading projects

   - 35 hours of project management education/training or their O2O CAPM(r) Certification

   OR

   - A high school diploma or an associate's degree (or global equivalent) Associate degree is roughly 65 credits and your American Council of Education Credits on your VMET or your Joint Services Transcript (JST) may be considered.

   - 60-month leading projects

   - 35 hours of project management education/training or their O2O CAPM(r) Certification

   To obtain their Certified Associate Project Management (CAPM) certificate from O2O you must have:

- Secondary degree (high school diploma, associate's degree, or the global equivalent)
- 23 hours of project management education completed by the time you sit for the exam.

O2O Project Management Basics online course fulfills this educational prerequisite—see more at https://www.pmi.org/shop/p-/elearning/project-management-basics—-an-official-pmi-online-course/16125

To learn more about the PMP and how it can help with civilian careers see the https://vets2pm.com/blog/ for PMP veteran articles.

2. ***Six Sigma Belt Certifications***

Similar to level belts in martial arts classes, Six Sigma is broken down into six levels of mastery for learning Lean operating principles for businesses. The goal is to train the person in Lean thinking and effective utilization of Lean tools and principles that can improve projects, programs, and operations across multiple business platforms and models.

- Level 1 is White Belt: This level involves a single session where a person would learn the methods and terms for Lean Six Sigma. The training involves levels of an organization and how they contribute to the reliable end product or outcome. This level involves projects and problem-solving tasks.

- Level 2 is Yellow Belt: This level showcases the Six Sigma concepts in a one- to two-day training where the person would be assigned and involved in a limited-scope project to assist managers and operations.

- Level 3 is Green Belt Certification: This level is a certification process that requires a full course training and project showcase that explains the Six Sigma methods for improving products, services, and processes over a cycle. The person would learn about problem-solving frameworks, performance metrics, and business processes. The goal for this certification is to have used the leadership Lean tools throughout a full cycle of a project.

- Level 4 is Black Belt Certification: You must complete Green Belt Certification first to move on to Black Belt Certification training. In the training, the person will master the Lean Six Sigma skills of leading and expanding projects and organizational changes. The goal is to drive organizational changes, analyze the data, deploy Lean principles, and lead Green Belt level projects. Black Belt Certification requires the person to demonstrate what they learned and execute projects under the Lean Six Sigma method.

- Level 5 is Master Black Belt: Using Lean Six Sigma Principles throughout the business and across projects and teams, the Master Black Belt is a leader who has a proven record of problem-solving and project management driving organizational and business changes.

- Level 6 is Champion and is usually for upper-level managers who have led Lean Six Sigma objectives on the executive level throughout all of the business.

Most corporate and manufacturing employers want either Green or Black Belt Six Sigma Certification. Many military service members can easily obtain the Green or Black Belt certifications due to the level of projects and programs they work with and coordinate.

Many universities offer this training within their business or engineering programs. Some offer it as a certification course with college credits and others offer it as a professional development option.

List of some universities that offer it for active duty personnel for discount or free:

Purdue University: https://www.purdue.edu/leansixsigmaonline/

Syracuse University may offer **free** training through the O2O division: https://ivmf.syracuse.edu/programs/career-training/learning-pathways/

3. *IT/Coding/Security/Programming Courses*

Many computer training courses are offered for free to active-duty service members. Some caution to help in deciding where to gain your skillsets in computer science. If you do not plan to get a college degree in IT or Cybersecurity, then some programs are free to help train you in various IT careers. But if you plan on eventually getting a degree then look at colleges that offer IT certifications with college credit. This way you can add up the credits towards a degree.

Examples of free IT certifications

- American Military University offers active-duty the Freedom Grant option at https://start.amu.apus.edu/freedom-grant/overview?utm_source=military-base&utm_medium=banner&utm_content=freedom-grant&utm_campaign=AMU%20-%20DT%20-%20AMU to help them pay for their education at the school which has multiple certifications and degrees for IT and Cybersecurity.

- Syracuse University's O2O: https://ivmf.syracuse.edu/programs/career-training/learning-pathways/?q=/employment/vctp-certification-paths/&

- Veterans4quality: https://veterans4quality.org/

- Federal Virtual Training Environment through the Department of Homeland Security created free Cybersecurity training for veterans at https://fedvte.usalearning.gov/coursecat_external.php

- The USO is offering free training and certification tools for cybersecurity to active-duty and veterans at https://www.uso.org/skillsoft

- The VA offers technology education to veterans. You cannot be on active-duty to participate in this free tech offering. They offer training in software, programming, media applications, and data processing. Got to https://www.va.gov/education/about-gi-bill-benefits/how-to-use-benefits/vettec-high-tech-program/

- LinkedIn Premium training offers a variety of IT courses and they are free for one year at https://www.linkedin.com/pulse/free-training-certificates-veterans-daniel-stanton?articleId=6677908287037444096

- The USO grant allowed Google.org to create a free training certificate program for veterans and military spouses. Google IT Support Certificates at https://grow.google/programs/it-support/#?modal_active=none

4. *Technicians in Manufacturing, Logistics, and Quality Jobs*

Some schools and training programs offer free or significantly reduced certification and training to active-duty service members and veterans.

- DANTES offers certifications: https://www.dantes.doded.mil/

Some examples of schools and training programs that are free or reduced:

- The Manufacturing Institute: https://www.themanufacturinginstitute.org/veterans/heroes-make-america/training-program/
- IJCSA offers: Janitorial Master Level Certification: https://www.ijcsa.org/Janitorial-Certification-Program/
- Chemical Hazard Certification Program: https://www.ijcsa.org/Hazardous-Chemical-Certification/
- Green Cleaning Certification: https://www.ijcsa.org/Green-Cleaning-Certification/
- Hire Heroes offers training resources: https://www.hireheroesusa.org/training-partners/
- TEEX extension service from Tower Techs, Fire Science to Emergency Medical: https://teex.org/program/veterans-benefits/
- Supply Chain Certifications from LinkedIn Premium which is free for Active-Duty: https://www.linkedin.com/pulse/free-training-certificates-veterans-daniel-stanton?articleId=6677908287037444096

5. *Aviation Training/Certifications for All Fields*

Certifications from FAA-approved training schools to work in the civilian sector can be earned while serving.

Go to the www.faa.gov/licenses_certificates/airline_certification/

Also, go to their For Veterans (faa.gov) page at www.faa.gov/jobs/working_here/veterans/

Remember that the FAA regulations allow military veterans trained in aviation MOS to use their experiences to gain FAA certifications.

Example for of this sees the Overview of the Aviation Maintenance Profession (faa.gov).

You will need:

- DD-214
- JST: jst.doded.mil
- On the job training or training jackets details
- Any Military School certificates or records.

6. *Law Enforcement Certification*

See the manual provided by the Department of Justice for the transition from military to law enforcement at www.theiacp.org/sites/default/files/2018-08/VetsGuide_300dpi.pdf

7. *Human Resource Certification*

SHRM Certification and funding for eligible military and veteran professionals: https://www.shrm.org/certification/apply/eligibility-criteria/Pages/Military-Eligibility.aspx

HRCI (PHR) certification for Military HR Personnel: https://www.hrci.org/our-programs/certify-your-staff/certification-for-military-hr-personnel

IVMF at Syracuse University PHR and SPHR certification: https://ivmf.syracuse.edu/programs/career-training/learning-pathways/

For all certifications and licenses

See the book from the Department of Labor at Licensing and Certification for Veterans: State Strategies for Successfully Removing Barriers (dol.gov) at www.dol.gov/sites/dolgov/files/VETS/legacy/files/licensingcertfications.pdf

Many of the certifications, training, and schooling you will need to gain the career you desire can be accomplished while serving. Many times, training can be used for college credits and some training can be transferred to civilian certifications. Research all areas of the career and your current opportunities in the service before spending cash out of pocket for any of the training or certifications. Companies do benefit by hiring veterans and often they will offer training to supplement what you already learned in the military.

Also, call any companies you are interested in to find out if they offer training or expect certification before hiring.

Since we're looking at education options, are you rethinking transitioning now that you know more about the training/schooling only offered to active-duty?

My Decision on transition is to

_____

Confidence Meter: How Confident are you with your decision?

1 – 2—3—4—5—6—7—8—9—10

Unsure   Almost sure   Very Sure

Remember this decision is not a reality until you receive your DD-214. If you decide to wait and stay in the military, then tuck this book away until you are ready to transition. If you want to continue, head-on to the next chapter

FIFTH MONTH:

VMET AND JST

Month: _____

SUNDAY	MONDAY	TUESDAY	WEDNESDAY	THURSDAY	FRIDAY	SATURDAY

The objectives for Chapter Five:

- To understand the difference between VMET and JST

- To understand how these documents can aid in your employment search

- To decipher and use the information provided on each of these documents to help you in the civilian world.

The goal of this chapter is to help you uncover the skills, and training that your received in the military and to help you display those experience in your resume. In my experiences of working with veterans, I have found that they often short-change or dismiss their work experiences or skills, especially on resumes and in interviews. They leave out important day-to-day skills that civilian employers often desperately need or look for. Simple training and common knowledge in the military sector are not common in the civilian world. So, to offer this expertise or knowledge on your resume can make a difference in being interviewed over another.

The Verification of Military Experience and Training (VMET)

The VMET, also known as DD-2586, is a reported record of the servicemember's demographics, training, experiences, deployments, and acknowledgments. The report will list information including MOS, duty stations, deployments, certifications, training, service ribbons, badges, medals, and ranks from the day you start basic training till the last day of your service.

The following systems feed information to the VMET database about each service member's work experience and military training.

ARMY

- ATRRS (Army Training Requirements and Resource System)

- TAPDB (Total Army Personnel Database)

NAVY

- NITRAS (Navy Integrated Training Resources & Administration System)

- BUPERS (Bureau of Naval Personnel)

- OPINS (Officer Personnel Information System)

- NES (Navy Enlisted System)

- IMAPMIS (Integrated Manpower & Personnel Management Information System) - Occupation for Navy Reserve Only

MARINE CORPS

- MCTIMS (Marine Corps Information Management System)

- MCTFS (Marine Corps Total Force System)

AIR FORCE

- MilPDS (Military Personnel Data System)

To access the VMET document you must have one of these three credentials to log in:

- Current Common Access Card (CAC)
- DS Logon, Level 2
  - See https://www.dmdc.osd.mil/appj/dsaccessto learn how to obtain the DS Logon.

- Or VA e-benefit portal at https://www.ebenefits.va.gov/ebenefits-portal
- DFAS myPay LoginID and Password at https://mypay.dfas.mil.

To access your VMET sign into **milConnect** and Choose **DODTAP** (eForm and VMET) from the Correspondence/ Documentation tab. Then select VMET. The screen has many prompts before your VMET is visual.

Each branch has another method to access and obtain the VMET documents. Reservists or National Guard would follow the branch they are associated with on how to access their VMET outside of the milConnect site.

ARMY: Soldiers need the DFAS myPay account or a CAC card to access their VMET

NAVY: The Navy Fleet and Family Support Centers can help you obtain your VMET. Visit www.ffsp. navy.mil and click on FFSC locations to find a center.

MARINE CORPS: If you are on a joint base with the Navy, you can also go to the Navy Fleet and Family Support Centers to obtain your VMET. Also, you can contact the Transition Assistance Management Program (TAMP) at the local Career Resource Management Center or call the USMC Transition Support number at 703-784-9523 (DSN: 278-9523).

AIRFORCE: The Air Force Personnel Center (AFPC) is one place to obtain the VMET and if you are at a joint Naval Air Station you can also use the Navy Fleet and Family Support Centers.

COASTGUARD: The Coast Guard does not use the VMET database to record the service of their members. The Coast Guard's Military Record is called the Coast Guard Personnel Data Record or EI-PDR. To receive a copy of your EI-PDR you must send a digitally signed email with an SF_180 forum from the EMPLID using your USCG.MIL account. You will send this request to MR_CustomerService@ uscg.mil or faxed the SF_180 form to 202-372-8440. You can all 202-795-6375 if you need special arrangements to view your EI-PDR.

SPACE FORCE: As of January 2021, this program's information on transitioning has not been added to the milConnect site but currently it does fall under the AIR FORCE branch. **Please see https:// www.spaceforce.mil/ for future information for transitioning soldiers from this new branch of the military.**

Print the VMET for your records. You may have to print the VMET every six months before you transition just to verify the information and help write your Resume. If you have more than ten years of service, use the centers listed above to use their printers to print a copy. Some VMETS can be over 30 pages long.

What to Expect in Your VMET

The first nine items in this document are your demographics: Name, gender, SSI number, pay grade, branch, and component, date of birth, date of the VMET information last listing, current MOS and title, and the number of years of service.

The tenth item starts the Experience and training from the most current to the first MOS.

You will see the following subtitle for every MOS or Job Occupation throughout your VMET.

- **Occupation:**

- **Primary Occupation:**

- **Duty Occupation:**

- **Occupation Description**: (this includes pay grades descriptions)

- **Credit Recommendation from the American Council on Education**

- **Related Civil Occupations**

Check every section of the Experiences and Training with your binder of your certifications and information. As a service member, you are reminded to constantly keep your VMET current, complete, and official. The DMDC cannot update the VMET until they receive Branch of Service notification and validation of the data. They do hire investigators to ensure correct data information is displayed on your VMET. Also, they use systems that can take some time to process data. Sometimes when the government offices are closed the data may take longer to process. Keep a record of your accomplishments to match with the VMET. This VMET needs to be current before separating from the military. The DMDC processes data for the VMET quarterly so check for updates in February, May, August, and November.

If there is missing training or information about base-level programs check with your file that is with the CO and if it is from your current MOS, see if the Branch, base, or CO did not report it to the DMDC. Some MOS descriptions are not what you may exactly do or may not include other types of work you have done in that position. If this is so, write what is missing down near that MOS description for future use in the resume, but discuss with Command why the job description is brief. Most likely they used a code for the MOS that was written by the DOD for reporting. Only Command can change the code or description.

An example to showcase this is the Navy Quartermaster MOS which is very brief and does not reflect the entire job or duties on the job. The MOS describes "*Quartermasters (QM) stand watch as assistants to the Officer of the Deck (OOD) and the Navigator; serve as Steersmen; perform ship control, navigation, and bridge watch duties; procure, correct, use, and stow navigational and oceanographic publications and charts; maintain navigational instruments and keep correct navigational time, and render honors and ceremonies in accordance with national observances and foreign customs.*" (Navy COOL, 2021). But most Quartermasters will also explain that they must do other duties to ensure the ships are ready for deployment or that the staff is trained to go to sea. Most military personnel understand that the MOS job description is only a basic overhaul, but the realities of the duties mean that you will work overtime and do other jobs, and whatever else it takes to complete the mission. Because your VMET does not showcase everything you do, this does not mean you should not add those missing items to your resume when applying for a job. I recommend going through each MOS occupation description and add those duties that are missing on the VMET for your reference.

> *** A warning about civilian employment—the job description is an agreement between you and your employer, and it ensures that you are being paid for that work. Some civilian workers take this as fact and will not help or budge beyond the requirements listed in their job descriptions or help complete the job or work overtime. Many veterans will find this choice frustrating when working with these types of individuals. This work ethic lacks initiative and teamwork and can lower the morale, creating a negative environment at their place of work. Many employers recognize this and often reward veterans and those who take the initiative on the job to complete the tasks needed to make the business successful. The incentive for this initiative, the civilian world, overtime is paid and sometimes 2x the hourly rate.

The VMET will also showcase college credits by the American Council on Education (ACE). The ACE coordinates the nation's higher education. They evaluate certain military occupations and training for college translations and consideration of academic credits. So, after some of the training on your VMET you will see the ACE and several academic credit hours. This means they value the training to be equivalent to hours of college credit. See the ACE at https://www.acenet.edu for more information. Please note that the ACE does not evaluate the Air Force members' occupations or training because it is done by the Community College of the Air Force (CCAF). And the ACE has not evaluated some of the Marine Corps occupations as of January of 2021 according to the milconnect. dmdc.osd.mil website.

Joint Service Transcripts (JST)

The Joint Service Transcript translates the military experience into academic credit for civilian use. The JST can be sent to colleges outside of the military for use of transfer credit in a degree program. Also, the JST can be used on an employment application for those jobs that require some type of college credit or credit hours. Some government, law enforcement, and business require several college credits for consideration in employment and this is when your JST can be used. The JST can also be used to confirm and identify skills for a career path as well as to help develop your resume for applying to companies.

The JST is an additional document beyond your VMET. JST records all education and training that the service member participated in throughout their career in the military. It replaces the older transcript version used previously such as the SMART, AARTS, and the CGI databases.

The Air Force use their CCAF transcripts and it would be different than the JST used by the other branches.

The JST and the CCAF should match the information on your VMET.

To access these documents, see the following websites:

JST: https://jst.doded.mil/jst/

CCAF: https://www.airuniversity.af.edu/Barnes/CCAF/Display/Article/803247/community-college-of-the-air-force-transcripts/

Hard Versus Soft Skills

Hard skills are defined as abilities or skills that a person learned or acquired through classroom instruction, testing, or training. Hard skills would be listed on the resume and in the cover letter. Most hard skills are technical or trade-related.

Soft skills are personality traits, habits, and learned skills that define your character. Employers often prefer candidates who have stronger interpersonal skills over technical aptitude.

What Skills Can be Transferred from the Military to the Civilian?

The military provides both hard and soft skills training. The initial boot camp training creates a new series of hard and soft skills for service members that stay with them throughout their service. For this chapter, I want to focus on soft skills and what the military has created for you that will benefit you in the civilian world.

Below is a list of transferable soft skills that you may have acquired in your service. These skills can be used in your resume writing to define your experiences.

Put a checkmark (√) by the ones you have experience with:

- Adaptability Skills – Able to adapt to new situations, people, and environments

- Administrative Skills – Able to coordinate people, paperwork, and product

- Advanced Writing Skills – Able to write above eighth grade

- Advanced Computer Skills – Microsoft Office, Email, and Social Media knowledge

- Analytical and Logical Thinking Skills – Based on observation, you can draw upon specific conclusions

- Artistic Skills – Able to design and display material for print, video, or social media

- Attention to Detail – Aware of the issues and tasks needed to complete projects

- Care-giving Skills – Able to care for those in need; humanitarian efforts

- Coaching Skills – Ability to give constructive feedback and listen actively

- Conflict Resolution – Can find peaceful solutions in volatile situations

- Counseling Skills – Able to listen and respond to conversation, build trust and openness

- Critical Thinking Skills – Able to generate ideas, solutions, and weigh the pros and cons of a situation

- Crisis Response Skills – Able to assess a situation and analyze what supplies, gear, or tactics are needed to minimize damage or resistance; able to read the room

- Customer Service Skills – Can build trust and dialogue with clients, groups, and organizations vital to the mission

- Decision-making Skills – Can evaluate feasibility and select the most viable possibility/choice

- De-escalation skills – Ability to defuse a volatile situation

- Driven – Focused on completing a task, mission, or objective

- Endurance – Able to sustain physically, mentally, and emotionally in stressful situations or stamina which means to sustain prolonged effort in a project and continue until it is complete

- Financial Skills - Budgeting, mathematics, SOP, and project management/monitoring expenses

- Goal-oriented – Focused to complete tasks and can be relied upon to finish projects

- Interviewing Skills – Able to ask and respond to questions in an effective and thorough manner

- Interpersonal Skills – Able to interact and communicate with a diverse population

- Leadership Skills – Empowers and motivates others to succeed

- Language Skills – Bilingual or multilingual

- Mechanical Ability – Able to install, operate, and maintain equipment

- Mediation Skills – Can de-escalate conflict and resolve it in a positive manner

- Mentorship – Skilled in training, teaching, and educating others, providing constructive feedback

- Motivation – Inspire and successfully encourage others

- Negotiating Skills – Able to compromise or persuade others

- Nonviolent Crisis Intervention – Experience in de-escalating situations; conflict resolution expert

- Verbal Communication Skills – Public-speaking experience and comfortable around others

- Organizational Skills – Able to coordinate information, people, and things in a systematic way, can prioritize

- Persuading Skills – Communicates clearly and effectively to influence others or a decision

- Public speaking Skills – Able to present in front of others about important information or events

- Planning Skills- Able to plan programs, projects, and events to meet objectives and decisive on the best options

- Problem-solving Skills – Able to clarify problems and evaluate options/solutions, able to speak up and propose action items to solve an issue

- Performing Skills – Can engage in various media outlets to inform, persuade, and amuse others

- Perceptual Skills – Able to visual situations, objects, and estimate physical boundaries

- Professional Values – Being accountable, focused, driven, dedicated and reliable at work

- Research Skills – Able to search out information, analyze data, summarize findings, and write a report

- Resiliency – Capable of recovering quickly from difficult situations and events

- Self-starter – Able to self-motivate and pursue objectives, goals, and projects without interference or guidance from others

- Supervisory Skills – Can establish responsibilities for members of a team and hold them accountable through constructive feedback/leadership

- Task-oriented – dedicated to completing a mission, objective, or project.

- Teaching Skills – Able to train/educate others and to create an effective learning space

- Teamwork Skills – Works well with others

- Training Skills – Able to teach/mentor/educate others on a specific skill or trade

- Trouble-shooting-skills –Able to solve serious problems for a company/organization/division

- Technological Skills – Understand and can operate/maintain/fix technical equipment or systems

- Time-management Skills – Able to organize and plan specific divisions of time throughout the day to accomplish tasks.

- Work Ethic – Believes in the principle that hard work is virtuous and rewarding

Let us check in with our decision about separating from the military. This decision is about what is best for you and your loved one. By using this book, you are getting informed and prepared for a life-altering career move.

My Decision on transition is to

_____

Confidence Meter: How Confident are you with your decision?

1 – 2—3—4—5—6—7—8—9—10

Unsure   Almost sure   Very Sure

Remember this decision is not a reality until you receive your DD-214. If you decide to wait and stay in the military, then tuck this book away until you are ready to transition. If you want to continue, head-on to the next chapter

SIXTH MONTH:

DEFINING YOUR EXPERIENCES

Month: _____

SUNDAY	MONDAY	TUESDAY	WEDNESDAY	THURSDAY	FRIDAY	SATURDAY

The objectives for Chapter Six:

- To understand how to translate your military experience into civilian skills

- To understand the military experience and how it affects civilian opportunities

- To use decision-making tools and worksheets to help the transitioning military person understand their skill set for civilian opportunities

Now that we have looked at your VMET and JST plus you have gathered all your prior documents, certifications, and information from your binder, let us understand the career options you may have in the civilian world and how to develop your goals for civilian employment around them.

MOS Crosswalk

First, let us go through your VMET and list all your MOS occupations. Either write MOS ID or write the name of the occupation—it is up to you. Start with your more current MOS and work backward. I have 14 spots on this form, but most of you will have at least four different MOS occupations during your career with the military.

1. MOS: _____

2. MOS: _____

3. MOS: _____

4. MOS: _____

5. MOS: _____

6. MOS: _____

7. MOS: _____

8. MOS: _____

9. MOS: _____

10. MOS: _____

Next, let us look at the skills listed in each:

Go to the Occupation Descriptions listed in your VMET

Here is an example:

MOS Title: 92Y: Army Unit Supply Specialist for Food Service

The description on VMET and ArmyCPOL for Supply Technician/92Y:

Serves as a Supply Technician and Assistant System Administrator for the Army Food Management System (AFMIS) at an Installation Subsistence Supply Management Office (SSMO). Performs a variety of supply management functions. Serves as an advisor to the Subsistence Supply Manager on both functional and technical supply matters relevant to the operation of the SSMO and AFMIS.

Work includes requirement determination, short and long-range forecasting, distribution, and procurement methods. Maintains detailed records through the automated Army Food Management Information System (AFMIS). Prepares and processes financial transactions, receipt documents, and issues documents through an automated system. Reviews AFMIS generated Standard Army subsistence report listings to ensure accurate input of all garrison and field accounts. Establishes and maintains a variety of office files on all accounts. Determines quantities of subsistence items to be ordered through automated Army Food Management Information System (AFMIS). Requisitions subsistence items through the automated system Subsistence Total Ordering and Receipt Electronic System (STORES). Estimates troop strengths and computes requirements for perishable and semi-perishable items. Determines requirements by perishability of the item, storage conditions, issue and consumption cycle, and transportation schedules for delivery. Computes, compiles, and forwards information to establish contracts for dairy products, bakery goods, and beverages through the SSM to Defense Logistics Agency (DLA). Maintains liaison with prime vendor and DLA to adjust or change requisitions or transportation dates of requisitioned items. Provides information to customer's inquiries relative to items on order, delivery dates, or cancelations. Makes independent determination when notified by supply sources that items are not available, rejected due to poor quality, or not meeting government standards. Reviews inventory on hand, due-in quantities, and known requirements to determine what needs to be done, (e.g., substitutions, reorder or cancel requisitions). Provides advice and assistance to SSMO personnel, customers, and logistics personnel on established supply policies and procedures. Uses available resources and techniques to identify and retrieve required data for use in responding to customer queries. Provides assistance, as required, in both the functional and technical operations of the system. Interprets both functional user manual and technical material. Works with SSMO personnel to research and resolve supply problems. Maintains backup files for AFMIS and STORES. Computes the basic daily food allowance for the installation. Prepares the monthly schedule of subsistence issues and direct vendor delivery requirements. Assists in the preparation of reports to higher headquarters. Maintains contact with commercial vendors to validate requirements and to resolve billing errors or problems to facilitate payment. Contacts AFMIS point of contact or SMS for assistance when needed. Accomplishes clerical, statistical, and data entry tasks to support the administrative work of the office.

Some VMET descriptions are very detailed, as you can see from this example, and some are basic. It depends on the type of occupation. Anything to do with the Special Forces, Navy Seals, Army Rangers, pilots, radar, Space Force, IT, or current Warfare operations MOS descriptions will be censored until that war/mission/operation is concluded and cleared for the public knowledge. Remember if your MOS involves Secret Clearance or Confidentiality clauses you are not permitted to discuss your work duties or experiences in your resume, with an employer or in an interview. Many transitioning veterans who want to stay in the field that is censored will often seek out employment with the contractors/companies they currently work with, a business that manufactures the items they deal with, or with the government entities that work with the items or programs.

For example, radar operators will seek employment with the company that manufactures the radar.

I once worked back-to-back with HIMARS experienced soldiers when I was teaching the DOLEW workshops and all of them worked exclusively with this weapon in training and combat. Many of these soldiers were worried they could not find employment with this experience. So, for the ones who felt comfortable staying with the product as a civilian, I encouraged them to research the manufacturer. They found out the manufacturer for the HIMARS was hiring representatives for their company to oversee the training in various countries with various militaries. Then I asked them to discuss their experiences with contractors in the field. They were encouraged to research and find contractors who also were hiring trainers in the field for this weapon. And lastly, looking at government employment through the DOD that oversaw the reporting of the warfare using this weapon and they did find a federal opening looking for someone experienced with the use and dangers of firing this weapon to observe and work with the manufacturer. So do not believe for one second that your skills in the military are too difficult to find a civilian opportunity—your skills are needed and wanted regardless of what you did for the military.

Getting back to the Occupation Description, using my example above, I want to show you how to find your skills and experiences in your Occupation Description that can be used later on in your resume. The beautiful thing about the Occupation Description is that each sentence starts with a verb, which shows how the descriptive sentences in your resume that explain what you did should also start.

Example section:

Work includes requirement determination, short and long-range forecasting, distribution, and procurement methods. Maintains detailed records through the automated Army Food Management Information System (AFMIS). Prepares and processes financial transactions, receipt documents, and documents issued through an automated system. Reviews AFMIS generated Standard Army subsistence report listings to ensure accurate input of all garrison and field accounts. Establishes and maintains a variety of office files on all accounts.

Look at the skills:

Work includes requirement determination, **short and long-range forecasting, distribution, and procurement methods. Maintains detailed records** through the automated Army Food Management Information System (AFMIS). **Prepares and processes financial transactions, receipt documents, and issue documents through an automated system.** Reviews AFMIS generated Standard Army **subsistence report listings to ensure accurate input of all garrison and field accounts. Establishes and maintains a variety of office files on all accounts**.

On your future resume you could have under this occupation the following details and skills:

Supply Technician and Assistant System Administrator, Fort Drum, NY 2018-2020

- Determined short- and long-range forecasting, distribution, and procurement methods

- Maintained detail records through a Food Management automated system

- Prepared and processed financial transactions, receipt documentation, and issued documents through an automated system

- Reviewed Standard Army subsistence reporting listings to ensure accuracy of all accounts

- Established and maintained office files for all accounts.

Remember to use past tense on those verbs when writing a resume, regardless of whether you are still active. We will discuss resume writing in more detail in Chapter Eight.

Spend some time this month to go over each MOS and pull out the skills you acquired in each job and break it down as I did with the example above.

On the calendar at the beginning of this chapter, schedule time to do these breakdowns of your MOS occupations from your VMET.

Goal: Schedule three MOS descriptions from your VMET to break down a day until all our doing.

Translating Your Military Job Title into a Civilian Title

Most companies and industries label the same job by different titles. Some may use the word specialist instead of generalist or the working mechanic instead of the word for specialist. Just like the different branches of the military use different titles for the same type of occupation, so does the civilian world. Understanding what your job title is called in the civilian world will help you in writing your resume and searching for similar work in the civilian sector.

Some translations of titles from Military to civilian:

Army MOS 91B: Wheeled Vehicle Repairer

Civilian jobs that MOS skills can be used in Automotive Engineering Technician, Automotive Mechanic, Service Technician, Mobile Heavy Equipment Mechanic

Marine MOS 0352: Anti-tank Missileman

Civilian jobs that MOS skills can be used in: Security or First Line Law Enforcement, Hazardous Materials Specialist, Emergency Management Specialist

Navy MOS YN: Yeomen

Civilian jobs that MOS skills can be used in Administration, Clerks, Assistants, Secretaries, Managers, Project managers, Program Coordinators.

Air Force MOS 2A372: Integrated Avionics Systems Craftsman

Civilian jobs that MOS skills can be used in: Avionics technician, First line mechanic/repairer, aviation maintenance, aviation mechanic

Here are some websites that can help you learn the different titles for what your MOS in the military translates in civilian terminology:

O*NET Interest Profilers website provides a database of different occupations and even has a Military Occupation Codes Crosswalk tool that can take your MOS and translate it into various civilian careers that you could walk right into with your military experiences and training. This MOS Crosswalk can be found at www.onetonline.org/crosswalk/MOC

Veterans.gov has a different area you can investigate for job searches that provide occupational roles. Go to www.Veterans.gov and search under the Find a Job tab. Start with Explore Careers if you are unsure of what to look for. And yes, this site can connect you to a career coach.

TAOnline.com has an amazing MOS/AFSC/MOC Civilian Occupation Translator at www.taonline.com/mosdot.

CareerOnestop is a website sponsored by DOL American Job Centers and the Civilian to Military Occupation Translator at www.careeronestop.org/BusinessCenter/Toolkit/civilian-to-military-translator.aspx

Military Connection.com also supplies a MOS Translator for Civilian Occupation at http://military-connection.com/mos-translator/

Military.com has created a Military Skill translator at www.military.com/veteran-jobs/skills-translator

Google.org received a grant from the USO that created the MOS/MOC job search and civilian career translator. All you do is type your MOS code into the Google search engine and it should showcase civilian jobs that match your MOS.

Designing a Career Path

Now you have spent some time investigating what your military experience was and how you can translate it into a civilian career. But you may not be sure that is the path you want to take. Maybe we need to assess your interests, your strengths, and your values to see what careers may be in your next path. We all have a variety of occupations we can do, but based on our interests, personality, and values, only a few can make us fulfilled.

Let us take an interest assessment to see what the best path for your next career is.

Please go to CareerScope Assessment Portal at https://va.careerscope.net/gibill and click the green button that says New Evaluees Register Here. Set up an account with an email that you can access regularly.

Once registered you follow the prompts to take the 25-minute assessment.

This assessment will ask questions that will uncover your interests, aptitude, and values. The report generated from this assessment will provide you with a series of occupations that your interests and aptitude match. Many of you will see that this assessment is similar to the ASVAB you took to get into the military. This assessment is focused on civilian career occupations and now that you have experiences and more training behind you, your scores will be different than the ASVAB results from years ago.

I want to list other career assessment tools that can help you if you found the CareerScope did not provide you with the answers or results you had hoped for.

a. CareerMaze is an assessment tool that looks at vocational strengths and weaknesses, work styles, aptitudes, and interests to help you uncover the occupations that fit your personality. Takes 10 minutes to take but cost $24.95 and results are instant at www.careermaze.com

b. 123Test.com has a free Career Aptitude Test that follows Dr. John Holland's Code of Personality Types to help decipher your career path at www.123test.com/career-test/

c. Jung Typology Test for Career Interests by Humanmentrics.com is a great way to see what your personality tells you is good or bad in an occupation. Take the free test at www.humanmetrics.com/cgi-win/jtypes2.asp#questionnaire

d. MAPP Career Assessment only takes 22 minutes and will assess you based on 71 triads. The report sent to your email will guide and motivate you to see what careers are in your best interest. Go to this website: https://www.assessment.com/?Accnum=06-5329-000.00

e. Keirsey Temperament Sorter has 70 questions that are based on the Myers-Briggs Types and will help guide you in career assessment at https://profile.keirsey.com/#/b2c/assessment/start

f. 16 Personalities Career Test is based on Jung Typology. The test can be found at https://www.16personalities.com

g. Red Bull Wingfinder is a personalized career assessment that focuses on your strengths and aptitudes. This free assessment takes about 35 minutes to complete and can be found at https://www.redbull.com/int-en/wingfinder

h. CareerOnestop has a Skill matcher Assessment that can be useful to help you develop a career path or plan to educate yourself for future career paths. Go to https://www.careeronestop.org/Toolkit/Skills/skills-matcher.aspx

i. Truity uses a variety of assessments to help you find your perfect career. Each assessment gives you a report that clarifies the results and gives your help with career occupations. Go to https://www.truity.com

j. Career Explorer offers a 30-minute assessment that helps you look at your personality archetypes and matches you with career occupations. Go to https://www.careerexplorer.com/assessments/

k. Career Test is a 32-question test that helps you to identify jobs or sectors that suit your professional interests and aptitudes at www.test-and-go.com/en/testfree/signin/TO

Assessment Results

Now do not laugh at some of the options you may have received. Like I said earlier, we all have a variety of occupations we can do.

So, let us review the results.

List the top seven occupations that your assessments said are a great fit for your future career:

1. _____

2. _____

3. _____

4. _____

5. _____

6. _____

7. _____

In your top seven, how many of the occupations need further schooling, training, or certifications?

_____

Are there any of the occupations you can do right now based on your current skill set, education and training?

_____

I hope the assessments helped you focus on a few occupations that you can research and look into for future careers. Now let us look at occupational trends in the area you plan on locating to after the military.

My Next Move is the website to use that can help you seek career options, research the career industry, and even look up jobs by MOS in the civilian sectors. Please go to https://www.mynextmove.org/vets/

Using some of the occupations you discovered in the career assessments, search under key words area of the website to find out information on those careers.

**The Bright Outlook "Sunshine" icon means the occupation is deemed a rapidly growing career by the Department of Labor.

** The Star in the Blue square icon shows you what MOS/MOC these civilian occupations match.

Using the ONET Interest Profiler Assessment at https://www.mynextmove.org/explore/ip

you can even search the My Next Move career database by Realistic, Investigative, Artistic, Social, Enterprising, and Conventional.

Some Criteria to Consider

Location: Does your location have opportunities for this career choice?

How many companies in the area hire for this career choice?

Is the salary pay adequate to afford the cost of living for the location?

Cost of Living: Does the salary afford the cost of living for the area allow for a single income?

Is the cost of food, housing, gas, schools, and recreation at your current location meet your economic level based on your occupation's salary?

Advancement: Is this occupation able to advance or grow into something else?

Is this occupation viewed as a growing career field by the DOL?

Education: Does this occupation require more schooling or training to advance?

Is a college degree or graduate degree required for hire?

Some viewpoints on career fields and industries to also consider:

Aviation Industry: Do you plan on relocating if the company requires it?

Do you want to work international, national, local, or in cargo?

Do your military certifications meet civilian FAA certification standards?

Can you transfer your Military certifications and licensures into FAA ones before separating from the military?

Business or Corporate: Are you interested in gaining further degrees or certifications such as an MBA, PMI, SPHR, or Six Sigma Certifications?

What is your main career goal for going corporate?

Education/ROTC: Do you have a college degree and a teacher's certification?

Do you have plans to continue for a Master's, Principal, or other educational occupations?

If you have a desire to help the youth, have you coached or volunteered with a school, a community center, or church to work with children beforehand?

Law Enforcement: Have you had all the required training needed to apply for civilian gun permits, clearances to work with children, and have taken the classes on Emergency management, addiction, sexual assault and harassment, first aid, de-escalation, mediation, diversity acceptance, and trauma/PTSD awareness? Remember, law enforcement can also work for Corporate. Some companies have their own police force. The pay varies but many city police are paid less than sheriffs. Also, check out the VA police jobs for transitioning military at www.vacareers.va.gov/Careers/TransitioningMilitary/

Medical: Licensures, certifications, and training can be achieved and transferred from the military to civilian companies. The VA hospitals have a program that can bridge medically trained service members into a federal position with the VA after transitioning from the military. www.vacareers.va.gov/Careers/TransitioningMilitary/

Service Industry: Most services are trade-oriented and may offer apprenticeships to help train the transitioning military. Some groups offer housing, meals, tools, and even college credit for their apprenticeships. Check out the different companies, unions, and schools that are in the specific industry to see if they list apprenticeship opportunities. Also, look at the VA program website www.dol.gov/agencies/eta/apprenticeship

The hospitality industry often has a training program for their specific specialty. Some services will need licensures in some states, check out what is expected for this career field in the state you plan to move to.

DOD SkillBridge Program

The DOD first started this bridging program to help transition the military into federal positions in our government. Within the last ten years or so, the defense industry was invited to work with the transitioning military. And today, most industries/companies can register to be involved in helping transition military move before their termination date, into a position that gives them civilian work experience.

See DOD SkillBridge (usalearning.gov) at https://dodskillbridge.usalearning.gov

Some points to discuss about this program:

- Some non-profit groups state that they can help you with this program, but in the end it is up to you to secure the opportunity.

- You also need to work with your CO and gain approval to be excused from the current MOS to participate in this program.

- SkillBridge opportunity **does not guarantee** a job offer with the company after you separate from the military

- While in the SkillBridge program you are still active in the military and expected to act accordingly. You still would receive military compensation and benefits. Also, you still would report to your CO regularly. All of these factors need to be considered before applying for this program. Please look over **SkillBridge Program Participant Ethics Brief** at https://dodskillbridge.usalearning.gov/docs/SkillBridge-Program-Participant-Ethics-Brief-V2.pptx

- Retirees or special warfare transitioning military, please be advised that your expertise or specialty may be needed in the military. If your MOS overseas subordinates and has a variety of responsibilities, getting a CO to approve your leave for this program can be difficult. Some retirees go terminal six months before separating, in that circumstance, the opportunity may occur for you to participate in this program. Gauge your current MOS, talk to your CO, and see if this program can apply to your situation.

Guidelines for SkillBridge

- DOD SkillBridge program guidelines at https://dodskillbridge.usalearning.gov/docs/Announcement-Career-Skills-Program-JTESTAI-Program.pdf

- The active-duty servicemember must have at least 180 days of service left to apply for this program

- While in this program, the service member receives military compensation and benefits.

- While participating in this program, they are still active-duty military, still will report to duty station, and may be required to still wear a uniform to their civilian employer.

SkillBridge Program by Military Branch

- **Air Force: https://afvec.us.af.mil/afvec/skillbridge/welcome**

- **Army: https://home.army.mil/imcom/index.php/customers/career-skills-program**

- **Navy:** Before applying for the SkillBridge program or gaining command approval, review DOD Instruction 1322.29 and NAVADMIN 222/15 policy documents. Contact the Transition Office (Fleet and Family Support Center) for more information on the SkillBridge program and opportunities. Locate your Fleet and Family Support Center at https://www.basedirectory.com

- **Marines:** For more information on the SkillBridge Program, call your installation SkillBridge point of contact:

29 Palms (760) 830-6344,

MCB Hawaii (808) 257-2654

Camp Pendleton (760) 763-3249,

South Carolina (843)228-4574,

Cherry Point (252) 466-6759,

MCAS Yuma (928) 269-2034,

Henderson Hall (703) 614-9104,

Camp Lejeune - New River (910) 451-4201

Iwakuni DSN: 315 253-6161,

MARFORRES (504)697-8128,

Okinawa DSN: 315 645-3150,

MCAS Miramar (858) 577-1428,

MCB Quantico (703)784-4963,

MCRD San Diego (619) 524-1283,

MCLB Albany (229) 639-5278.

- **Coast Guard:** Contact your Transition/Relocation Manager at the Office of Work-Life Programs to discuss the SkillBridge program https://www.dcms.uscg.mil/Our-Organization/Assistant-Commandant-for-Human-Resources-CG-1/Health-Safety-and-Work-Life-CG-11/Office-of-Work-Life-CG-111/Transition-Assistance-Program/TAP-Contact/

Military Pathways Programs

The first Pathway programs were designed by the DOD to get valuable veterans into federal government positions. The goal was the recruitment of these veterans before transitioning from the Military. The United States Office of Personnel Management has a 47-page handbook that explains the programs that the federal government funds to help different groups seek positions with the federal government. https://www.opm.gov/policy-data-oversight/hiring-information/students-recent-graduates/reference-materials/pathways-programs-handbook.pdf

The Pathway program was designed to have each division offer some program that would help recruit eligible candidates before graduating college or exiting the military. The VA Pathway Program is great for anyone wanting to work with the veteran population. https://www.va.gov/EMPLOYEE/pathways-program-requirements/

Corporations such as Amazon, JP Morgan, Bank of America, Lockheed Martin, and others create a military pathway program that would bring veterans on board through a training program and then have them work in that position until fully hired by the company. Similar to SkillBridge but usually requires college degrees and is used for management type of positions.

See Amazon's Military Pathway Program at https://amazon.jobs/en/jobs/1194531/military-pathways-2021-nationwide-opportunities-united-states

Junior Military Officer (JMO) Transition Programs

Civilian opportunities exist for Military officers with college degrees because of their leadership training. Some of the civilian careers that a JMO would transition to include:

- Quality or processing engineering
- Supervisors of logistics, supply chain or transportation
- Project management
- Program coordinator
- Operations or manufacturing business manager
- Sales manager.

Many recruiting firms will seek out a JMO candidate's resume. I still recommend talking with these specialized firms but also do your search as well. Below I will list some of the companies that participate in a JMO program for management for you to contact and submit your resume.

Also, look at this amazing page with a list of various companies that will work with the JMO program, Skill Bridge and Military Pathways. This organization is a veteran volunteer community who designed their website "The Patriots Initiative". Look at their Warriors in Transition page at https://www.thepatriotsinitiative.org/transition/warriorsintransition/

Some of the corporations that offer JMO programs for management and that have an excellent track record of hiring veterans in management roles:

- Amazon at https://www.amazondelivers.jobs/about/military/ or https://www.amazonfulfillmentcareers.com/opportunities/military/

- BAE Systems at https://jobs.baesystems.com/global/en/militaryveterans

- Bank of America at https://militarytransition.bankofamerica.com/

- Baker Hughes at https://public.bakerhughes.com/Military/

- BNSF at https://jobs.bnsf.com/go/Transitioning-Military/400926/

- Boeing at https://jobs.boeing.com/veterans

- Caterpillar at https://www.caterpillar.com/en/careers/career-areas/military.html

- Cummins at https://cummins-veterans.jobs/jobs/

- Cigna at https://jobs.cigna.com/us/en/militaryandveterans

- Cintas at https://careers.cintas.com/content/Military-and-Veteran/?locale=en_US

- Citigroup at https://www.citigroup.com/citi/citizen/community/citisalutes/working-jobs.html

- Exxon at https://veterans.exxonmobil.com/

- FedEx Freight at https://fedexfreight-veterans.jobs

- Ford Motor at https://corporate.ford.com/careers/transitioning-military.html

- General Electric at https://jobs.gecareers.com/global/en/veterans

- Halliburton at https://jobs.halliburton.com/content/veterans/

- Hewitt-Packard at https://www8.hp.com/us/en/jobs/veterans.html

- Honeywell at https://www.careersathoneywell.com/en/who-we-hire/transitioning-military/

- Leidos at https://www.leidos.com/operation-mvp

- Lockheed Martin at https://www.lockheedmartinjobs.com/military

- Logistic Health at https://lhicareers.com/veteran-resources.aspx

- Lowe's at https://corporate.lowes.com/careers/military

- Microsoft at https://military.microsoft.com/

- Northrop Grumman at https://www.northropgrumman.com/careers/veterans-transitioning-to-civilian-careers-job-search-and-networking-strategies/

- Raytheon at https://jobs.rtx.com/transiting-military

- Shell at https://www.shell.us/careers/military-veterans.html

- Southwest Airlines at https://careers.southwestair.com/military

- Textron at https://www.textron.com/Careers/Military-Veterans

- Union Pacific Railroad at https://up.jobs/military/index.htm

- Walmart at https://www.walmartcareerswithamission.com/content/people-experience/military.htm

- 3M at https://www.3m.com/3M/en_US/careers-us/working-at-3m/military-and-veterans/

- 7 Eleven at https://careers.7-eleven.com/careers/military-veterans

Let us check in with your decision:

My Decision on transition is to

_____

Confidence Meter: How Confident are you with your decision?

$$1 - 2—3—4—5—6—7—8—9—10$$

Unsure   Almost sure   Very Sure

Remember this decision is not a reality until you receive your DD-214. If you decide to wait and stay in the military, then tuck this book away until you are ready to transition. If you want to continue, head-on to the next chapter

SEVENTH MONTH:

PLANNING YOUR TRANSITION

Month: _____

SUNDAY	MONDAY	TUESDAY	WEDNESDAY	THURSDAY	FRIDAY	SATURDAY

The objectives of Chapter Seven

- Is to recheck our plan and check off the items we already completed for separation

- Also, reminders for items that need to be completed for termination from the military

The first six months of the start of your transition, you should have started gathering your experiences into one area. Using the previous activity where we looked at your VMET occupations to discover skills you can list on a resume. This month you will regroup and look at the entire TAP process to make sure we have taken into account everything you need to do to separate or retire from the military.

Desired Plan

First, let us look at the desired plan for transitioning from the military:

Fill in the areas to the best of your knowledge

Desired separation year and month: _____

Title of Desired Civilian Career _____

Desired Civilian Pay: _____ per year

Required Civilian Pay: _____ per month to meet lifestyle and family needs

Desired location to transition to: _____

Factors that Contribute to Your Plan

Now let us look at factors that help us get this plan finalized:

1. The family:

    Discuss with the members of your family who would be impacted by your transition the following items:

    Ask for their input on your separation from the military:

    A. What did they enjoy about being a part of your military experience?

    B. What did they dislike about the experience?

    C. What expectation did they have about the transition?

    D. Career-related: Do they assume you will be more readily available?

E. If they are supporting your departure from the military, why?

F. Do they believe you will have more stability/regular hours as a civilian?

G. Location – where do they want to live?

2. Finances in Order:

As you begin to adjust to the spending habits of a civilian, are you prepared to take over the military benefit areas not covered in civilian life?

A. Budget your money: Do you know where your money goes every pay?

B. Living like a civilian: Use one month while still active and live within a civilian budget. Put the money you would have to pay for living, food, and necessities into an envelope or a savings account…see what is left over after the month. Do you see where you need to cut, save or prepare to be when you leave the military?

C. Have you talked to financial counselors, insurance people, and credit card companies as suggested in Chapter 2?

D. Relocation, house selling/buying, moving trucks, and funds for travel. Is there a fund started to prepare for this move after transitioning?

3. Education/Training:

As you start to think about your future civilian career, will you need more training or skills to obtain the desired positions or career?

A. What skills, education, or certifications will you need? (If you do not know yet, do not worry we will discover those items in another chapter)

B. Are there any schools/programs you can attend now while active? What are they?

C. Time Management: Can you balance work, life, family, and school? And why?

D. What obstacles to completing your education/training are you facing, if any?

4. Medical:

Every service member will be cleared by their medical doctor at the VA hospital before separating from the service.

A. Have you scheduled all your appointments, filled out all your papers, and allocated time to learn more about disability, medical assistance, and occupational rehabilitation (if needed) job placements assistance?

B. Medical Insurance: Have you investigated Cobra or continued medical insurance after separating from your family?

C. Schedule to have the family receive all their medical checkups, dentist, and eye appointments before separating.

D. This is the time to discuss with your VA doctor any illnesses, injuries, mental or physical ailments you are experiencing. Since you know you are separating, this is the time to speak up and get the help you will need to be a whole and complete person in the civilian world. Most ailments can get treatments that are life-saving, so speak up now.

5. Transportation:

Determine if you will need to purchase new transportation for you or your family to access employment, medical services, or schools once leaving the military. For those who live on base, transportation may be the last thing you would think about, but it is essential and often necessary to have in the civilian world.

6. Mentors/counselors/peer support:

Most veterans want an outlet, someone, or something to help them adjust to civilian life. Today with social media and with so many organizations willing to support and serve the military service members, many veterans can find a group that will know exactly how they are feeling and what their experiences are while transitioning. The service member does not have to face any of their obstacles alone. Here is a partial list of groups, organizations, and social media outlets for veterans in the civilian world:

Marines for Life Network: A great social media group that connects Marines from all corners of the earth. They often post meet-ups in different cities, workshops, events and offer virtual groups, calls, and mentoring. https://usmc-mccs.org/services/career/marine-for-life-network/

Veterati: Mentorship platform that helps veterans and active-duty find mentors in many different fields to talk to for free. https://veterati.com

American Corporate Partners (ACP)- Mentorship helps active-duty veterans with transition www.acp-usa.org

Candorful – Mentorship for transitioning military https://candorful.org

RallyPoint: Active-duty and veterans can use this platform to discuss military life, experiences and share information https://rallypoint.com

VetFriends: Connecting Veterans through an online platform, events, and a protected database https://vetfriends.com

The Military Network: Organization for veterans from all military branches who mentor in career. https://linkedin.com/company/military-network-llc

Military Talent Partners: This organization works through mentorship and career counseling/coaching. https://militarytalentpartners.com

Militarygamers.com – An online community dedicated to serving military gamers from all branches. A fun site to connect with others

Also remember any of the American Legions, Veterans of Foreign Wars, and even the VA have supportive mentors that can assist a veteran in transitioning,

For more listing of organizations that work with veterans please look at Veteran Support Organizations (defense.gov) at www.defense.gov/Resources/Veteran-Support-Organizations/

To help you navigate all the different groups, here is a list of some questions you should research or ask before becoming a member of any organization or social club:

1. What is the mission of the organization and does it align with my core values and needs?

2. What kind of services do they offer?

3. Is there a fee tied to any of the services or memberships? (Many are free because they receive grants or donations but always ask before signing up.)

4. What is the value of being a member of this group or organization? Do they offer discounts, scholarships, career or financial counseling, human services, and do they volunteer in the community?

5. Does the organization have a local chapter, office, or center you can visit or attend?

6. Do they have a large following/membership and a good reputation?

7. Are they politically tied to anyone or a group? And do their political affiliations affect your own?

8. Is there religious tolerance or is the group tied to a religious entity or belief?

9. Is there diversity in the organization? Is the organization safe and open to other races, genders, and sexual orientations?

10. Are you comfortable with your name and face being connected to this organization, social media network, or club?

Now that we went over the major areas that go into your transition plan, let us ask once again about how you feel about your decision:

My Decision on transition is to

_____

Confidence Meter: How Confident are you with your decision?

1 – 2—3—4—5—6—7—8—9—10

Unsure   Almost sure   Very Sure

Remember this decision is not a reality until you receive your DD-214. If you decide to wait and stay in the military, then tuck this book away until you are ready to transition. If you want to continue, head-on to the next chapter

EIGHTH MONTH:

RESUME DEVELOPMENT

Month: _____

SUNDAY	MONDAY	TUESDAY	WEDNESDAY	THURSDAY	FRIDAY	SATURDAY

The objective for Chapter Eight:

- To learn what a resume is and how to create one for job applications

- To understand the different types and formats of a resume

- To learn the guidelines and rules of an Applicant Tracking System (ATS) resume and others.

Resume Development

What is a Resume?

Webster's dictionary defines a resume as being "a short account of one's career and qualifications or a set of accomplishments." (Merriam-Webster.com, 2021)

How many different resumes are there?

Depending on the career focus, the situation, the company's hiring method of receiving resumes, and the required skills to match the job description, these elements will dictate what kind of resume you will use.

Here is the basic list of the different types of resumes we will discuss in the following chapters:

Master Resume

This resume will not be sent to any job but is the total sum of your work. This resume lists every skill, education, job, training, volunteering, and work you have done up to the present-day. The reason you will not submit this type of resume is that you will build a specifically geared resume for the jobs you are applying for. You will use the Master resume's information in building those job-specific resumes. The benefit of first completing a Master Resume is that it provides you with everything you need to make a job-specific resume. And many of you will be sending out at least 10 to 15 resumes before finding the right employment.

Job Fair Resume

You will need several different types of resumes to take to a job fair. Many of you have several different career paths you could follow. For example, if you worked as an aviation mechanic but also did six years as a recruiter, you will have several resumes: one showcasing your aviation experience, a resume showcasing your mechanic experiences, a resume showcasing your recruiting experience, and a resume with all experiences. Job Fairs host a variety of different types of employment and opportunities. Narrowing your options by only providing one type of resume, can be frustrating and disappointing for job seekers. Keeping several options to pitch yourself gives you more opportunities.

Also, job fairs will need a one-page resume and a regular two- or more-page resume. Some recruiters at job fairs only have 30 seconds to talk with you; by providing a one-page highlighted resume upfront but then handing them also the detailed resume, allows the recruiter to focus on your words and write information down on the backside of the one-page resume but still have the full resume for their review.

Applicant Tracking System (ATS) Resume

Most companies ask for resumes through their online platforms. The computer system used to filter those resumes rely on coding to decipher and trim the resumes for the Human Resource Manager. Coding is very particular on what they will accept. This means that the resume will have to be formatted based on the ATS that the company is using. ATS resumes do not look pretty and they are not colorful. The coding will not recognize images, large font, colors, and columns. We will discuss this resume later in this chapter.

Resume Services

Resume writing businesses will be available to help you. The Veteran Non-Profits and Government organizations offer FREE services for Transitioning veterans. The resume developers and career counselors are certified to help veterans with job searches, resume writing, and cover letter writing. These are FREE. To find one of these organizations see the American Job Centers in your local area. https://www.careeronestop.org/localhelp/americanjobcenters/find-american-job-centers.aspx

Paid resume services can range from $50 to $500 or more per resume. Remember resumes need to be tailored for the job in which one is applying. Spending money on every resume that needs to be written can become costly. Using the same resume for each job limits the opportunities for interviews. If you choose to go with the paid version, please do your homework on the company.

1. They should be certified or educated in the career field.

2. Seek out reviews of the company's service—how many people got jobs from using their services.

3. Did not fall for over-the-top claims. IF they guarantee an interview, most likely they are using methods that could keep you from getting the job.

    Example of disreputable practices in the resume world.

    Let us look at the disreputable practice of using white font in the background of a resume that showcases keywords from a job description. I want to give a scenario of this practice:

    Say a veteran only had experience working on the F-22 aircraft and he finds a resume company that guarantees he will get an interview. They find him a job that works on aircraft but asks for F-35 experience.

    Despite not having that F-35 experience, he allowed the company to submit his resume. The company charged him over $290 to create the resume for the F-35 job. Within a week he does get an interview with the aviation manufacturer. During the interview he is told his resume was withdrawn from consideration for attempting to manipulate the ATS.

    The paid resume company used the white font in the background of his resume in order to add to the keyword count in the ATS system. Despite his resume only showcasing F-22 experience in Black font, the resume company used white font to repeat F-35 throughout the resume.

The resume company did what it claimed to do and got the man an interview. But the HR department at the aviation manufacturer was aware of this practice. Unfortunately, the man lost his opportunity to work with a great company because of this disreputable practice

Research the resume company, read reviews of their services and reputation before you sign or pay anything. Make sure they have a good reputation and success in helping people gain employment with their resumes.

4. Work with the resume writer so you know what is on the resume. Never let a resume be written that is not about your skills or your experience. In the interview, they will question you on what is written in the resume, about the experiences, education, and products/skills. Make sure what is written in the resume is something you can confidently discuss.

Understanding Resumes

Length

Unless the directions for the application state two pages or one-page, the length of the resume can be longer than two pages. Someone with 30 years of experience in a specific career field will have a minimum of three pages. Now many recruiters will state otherwise, but if you have more than 20 years of experience in a field, then your resume should showcase those experiences geared to match the job description.

Key Words

The most valuable items in your resume will be the keywords from the job description. You need the job description with you when creating your resume for a job opening. Highlight the keywords in that job description, especially anything repeated twice. Your resume should include the keywords or specific descriptions from the job opening that matches your skillset. This is crucial for military service members because the titles and names of jobs in the military are not the same in the civilian sector. Match your job title to the name on the job.

Example A:
Navy title: Aviation Boatswain's Mate
Civilian title from American Airlines: Ground Support or Fleet Service Agent
On resume use: Ground Support- Fleet Service Agent (Aviation Boatswain's Mate)

Example B:
Army MOS 90A: Logistics Officer.
Civilian title from Lockheed Martin: Logistics Coordinator, Logistics Analyst,
or Logistics Specialist Associate
On resume use: Logistic Coordinator/Analyst (Logistics Officer)

Images

Some resume designers and Word templates will suggest having images or a photo to add to your resume. Based on the Equal Opportunity Employment laws and policies, Human Resource managers are not allowed to accept or view any resumes with images/photos of the candidate on them. So, photos of yourself on a resume should be avoided.

Lines, boxes, symbols, monograms, or any form of graphics should also be avoided in ATS resumes. The coding software will automatically reject the resume due to the blocks of the image. Save the designer details for the job fair resume or an emailed or hand-delivered resume.

If the job application is sent to an email address, then use the designed resume but send it as a PDF so the images do not move the font.

What are the Different Formats for Resumes?

Chronological Resumes

Resume training before 2000 focused mainly on chronological formatting of information. Many colleges still teach this format as the main type of resume to present to an employer. In chronological, the education and work experience starts with the most recent and ends with the first job or degree. Also, in chronological, skills and details of jobs are less visible, but dates and locations are more prevalent. If there is a job gap, the resume will show this. Be mindful of any gaps in education, training, service, or work when choosing this format. For someone with a lot of experience or education, this format works well. Researching the company and its focus will help you when applying to decide if this format or any of the others is the best one to submit.

Example:
John Smith
1234 Transition Way
Arlington, VA
(888)111-1111
Johnsmith1234@gmail.com

Professional Summary: Logistical Specialist with 10 years of experience supporting international and domestic transportation, supply chain, and analysis to multiple military and civilian operations and companies. Led the development of sufficient inventory control, data analyst, warehouse, and supply chain management. Managed supply chain and logistics procedures to streamline all processes. Able to deliver materials in various conditions and constraints. Leader in coordinating internal and external departments to ensure delivery of material led to a successful operation.

Education:

Bachelor of Science, American Military University, Charles Town, WV, 2018

Major: Transportation & Logistics,

Employment Experiences:

US Army, Fort Sill, OK   2016-Present

Title: Supply and Logistics Manager

- Managed the shipping of over $15 million dollars in property, equipment and supplies to international and domestic locations.

- Trained, scheduled and monitored a unit of 7 logistic specialists

- Established and maintained various documents, reports and followed federal, military, and civilian regulation forms.

- Reviewed contracts, purchase requests, and shipping documents to verify the actual quantities received a match.

US Army, Fort Braggs, NC   2012-2016

Title: Logistics Specialist

- Reviewed contracts, purchase requests, and shipping documents to verify the actual quantities received a match.

US Army, Korea,   2010-2012

Title: Stock Clerk

Functional Resumes

The Functional resume focuses on skills, training, and experiences. This format is ideal for someone with little or no work experience but has acquired skills through their education and training. Also, this format is ideal for a trade applicant who wants the company to see their skills, training, and experiences in that particular field.

Example:
John Smith
1234 Transition Way
Arlington, VA
(888)111-1111
JohnSmith1234@gmail.com

Professional Summary: Logistical Specialist with 10 years of experience supporting international and domestic transportation, supply chain, and analysis to multiple military and civilian operations and companies. Led the development of sufficient inventory control, data analyst, warehouse, and supply chain management. Managed supply chain and logistics procedures to streamline all processes. Able to deliver materials in various conditions and constraints. Leader in coordinating internal and external departments to ensure delivery of material led to a successful operation.

Experiences:

- Managed the shipping of over $15 million dollars in property, equipment and supplies to international and domestic locations.

- Established and maintained various documents and reports, and followed federal, military, and civilian regulation forms.

- Trained, scheduled and monitored a unit of 7 logistic specialists

- Trained personnel in hazmat, osha, international and domestic inventory, and documentation for shipping.

- Maintained records and correspondence for a variety of operations and projects

- Reviewed contracts, purchase requests, and shipping documents to verify the actual quantities received a match.

- Reviewed contracts, purchase requests, and shipping documents to verify the actual quantities received a match.

- Proficient in Microsoft programs such as Excel, Power Point and Word

- SAP knowledge

- Coordinating dispatching, routing and tracking of all materials for several divisions globally.

Employment:

US Army, Supply and Logistics Manager Fort Sill, OK	2016-Present
US Army, Logistic Specialist, Fort Braggs, NC	2012-2016
US Army, Stick Clerk, Korea,	2010-2012

Education:

Bachelor of Science, American Military University, Charles Town, WV, 2018

Major: Transportation & Logistics

Combined Resumes

Combining chronological format with functional is considered the best type of resume to submit. The employer can learn about the length of employment, the types of education or training, and see the skill set/proficiency of the trade or career focus. This resume is usually three pages long or more.

Example:
John Smith
1234 Transition Way
Arlington, VA
(888)111-1111
Johnsmith1234@gmail.com

Professional Summary: Logistical Specialist with 10 years of experience supporting international and domestic transportation, supply chain, and analysis to multiple military and civilian operations and companies. Led the development of sufficient inventory control, data analyst, warehouse, and supply chain management. Managed supply chain and logistics procedures to streamline all processes. Able to deliver materials in various conditions and constraints. Leader in coordinating internal and external departments to ensure delivery of material led to a successful operation.

Experience:

US Army, Fort Sill, OK   2016-Present

Title: Supply and Logistics Manager

- Managed the shipping of over $15 million dollars in property, equipment and supplies to international and domestic locations.

- Established and maintained various documents and reports, and followed federal, military, and civilian regulation forms.

- Trained, scheduled and monitored a unit of 7 logistic specialists

- Trained personnel in hazmat, osha, international and domestic inventory, and documentation for shipping.

US Army, Fort Braggs, NC   2012-2016

Title: Logistic Specialist

- Maintained records and correspondence for a variety of operations and projects

- Reviewed contracts, purchase requests, and shipping documents to verify the actual quantities received a match.

- Reviewed contracts, purchase requests, and shipping documents to verify the actual quantities received a match.

US Army, Korea,   2010-2012

Title: Stock Clerk

- Proficient in Microsoft programs such as Excel, Power Point and Word
- SAP knowledge
- Coordinating dispatching, routing and tracking of all materials for several divisions globally.

Education:

Bachelor of Science, American Military University, Charles Town, WV, 2018

Major: Transportation & Logistics

Training/Skills

    Hazmat Training

    International and Domestic Trade

    Inspection

    Cost Reduction

    Work Schedules

    Troubleshooting/Maintenance

Targeted/Key Word Resumes

Targeted resumes can be any of the three formatted types (Chronological, Functional or Combined) as long as it is written to match a particular job or employer. The resume will showcase only the skills and job experiences that are geared to agree with the job description.

    This resume will list the skills that match the key skills of the job description.

Resume Guidelines

Depending on what format of a resume you will design, plus how you plan on submitting your resume, there are some rules.

Font

Resumes need to use a legible font. Stay away from italics, cursive, or capitalization styles in your resume.

Examples of some styles that are accepted:

Font Size

For ATS resumes the font size can only be between 10–12. Anything bigger will be thrown out of the system due to the coding. Anything smaller may be missed. For Job fairs or face-to-face submission, the font should be size 12 and you can emphasize your first name by going up to size 14 or 16. If you go bigger than 16 size font, make sure the reasons are not to use up space.

Columns

For ATS resumes only use one-column resumes. Coding will dismiss the information in the second column if you do submit a two-column in your online submission.

For one-page job fair resumes, use two columns and list your skills in the left column of your paper.

The "E" or "F" Pattern Viewing

The eye pattern of people reading English often scans documents from either an "E" or "F" pattern. When making designing your resume remember to add the KEY information in those areas.

Alignment

Based on the "E" or "F" patterns, set your resume on left-alignment. The heading (name, address, phone number, and email) can be aligned in the center but that should be the only information not left-aligned.

Bold, *Italics*, and <u>Underlines</u>

A resume should only use these items sparingly or never. Only **Bold** specific keyword information, your heading, and subtitles. Only use *italics* when posting a word not in English. It is very hard to read text in *italics,* especially at a job fair when you only have 30 seconds to impress a recruiter. And never use Underline on ATS resumes because the coding will not read it.

White Space

A carefully planned resume will possess white space. White space can be beneficial and allows the HR manager to have space to write notes. Also, in ATS submissions, white space allows coding to focus on the content. But a warning–too much white space can send the wrong message about skill set and experience.

Saving Formats

The various formats are .doc, .docx, .rtf and .pdf. If you are using the ATS or Online submission for a job, use the .rtf or .doc to submit the resume. Sometimes the company will list the type of format they need for their ATS system. Do not use PDF for ATS systems but do use PDFs for email submissions.

References

Do not add any mention to references on your resume. Do not add "References upon request" or any form of this statement on your resume. References should be on a separate paper ready to send when asked for by the recruiter or HR Manager.

Parts of a Resume

Every resume has parts or sections of information that should be visible to the HR Manager/Recruiter.

The Heading

This section is the most important of the entire resume.

What **DOES** go in this section:

Full name: Use the name that matches your driver's license for ID purposes—never use nicknames, abbreviated names, or Americanized versions of your name on a resume that the company will use to identify you.

Address: Due to military moves, it is okay to just have a current residing city and state without having a full address. Also, if you want to post your resume to social media outlets like LinkedIn then take off the full address and only have the city and state you want to gain employment in. If you have yet to move to your desired city, you can still add the city and state as your address but let them know you are moving after separating from the military. Some employers will pay for relocation, so check if the company will give assistance to relocate before adding a desired city and state.

Phone number: Make sure the number you give has a voicemail that is active and states your full name. Also, make sure your phone is available and charged. If you give a landline number, make sure it has an answering machine that states your full name. If other family members answer your phone, make sure they are aware you applied for a job so as not to ruin your chances of getting an interview. If you have more than one phone, you can list both but designate the main number or that one is a cell phone.

Email: Never use a nicknamed email account or work email account. Also, if you still have a Hotmail.com or aol.com email, you need to update it. Create an email that has your first and last name in it. Gmail tends to be a popular email company that employers are aware of.

Also, you can add:

LinkedIn URL a Business/Career website URL or other Business/Job-related communication links.

What **DOES NOT** go in this section:

- Photo of yourself

- Social Security information

- Demographics: Married, Gender, Age, Religion, Race

- Social Media that is not business-related: Snapchat, Facebook, Twitter, Instagram, TikTok, or a Tinder Profile link

- Political Affiliation

Objective:

Rarely used in resumes anymore. Considered outdated. The objective usually states what you want or desire for a job from the employer. Most employers look at resumes to see all the places they could use the candidate. The objective statement can be limiting and restricts the opportunities for you. The only places objective statement would be beneficial is for Federal and State job applications on resumes when applying to the specific job orders.

Professional summary:

A resume summary of your experience, skills, and achievements in a paragraph, positioned under the heading of your resume. The goal of this summary is to explain your skills and qualifications for the job you are applying for in 3–5 sentences. The summary is written to convince the HR Manager to read the entire resume to learn more about you.

Remember the "E" and "F" pattern scanning, the professional summary lies in the first scan area. If the key-words from the job are highlighted in the summary, the manager may continue to read the entire resume.

Examples:

Professional Summary:

Detailed-oriented Navy veteran with over 20 years of experience in administration, accounting, human resources, marketing, and operational office management. Proficient in Microsoft Office, Records Management, Government contracts, and budget. Excellent organization, public relations, and multi-tasking skills to handle large and time-sensitive projects and programs across multiple departments and groups.

Professional Summary:

US Army Logistical Specialist with over 10 years of experience delivering wide-ranging logistical and transportation support. Managed multiple military organizations and operations. Experienced in inventory control, data analyst, warehouse, and supply chain management. Able to initiate supply chain and logistics methodologies to streamline operations and processes. Highly skilled at directing multi-faceted logistics functions under strenuous time constraints. Expertise in coordinating cross-functional internal and external product and service delivery for domestic and international customers.

Professional Summary:

Experienced Aviation service technician/mechanic with over 10 years in commercial and military aircraft ground support, engine maintenance, and safety inspector experience. Worked in domestic and international sectors of the aviation industry. Experience with F404-GE-400/402 engines, fuel systems, and secondary power systems. Accountable for all areas of inspection on the aircraft, corrosion control, refuel, de-fuel, and training of subordinates.

Education Section

Before 2010, many employers ranked schools in career decisions. Where you received your degree was considered a deciding factor in the job placement. But with the onset of training and schooling online, this view has been outdated. Now employers are looking for students to work in the field while studying the career topic, And online schooling provides working college students the advantage over traditional college students. Traditional student usually go to school first for four years and then work. Online school now allows working adults to go back to school to gain the degree. Employers now realize that students who also have real work experience in the career field usually means a better-trained candidate. The military provides both real world experience and educational opportunities.

When formatting your education, you can set it up in a variety of different ways:

Version 1:
Name of school. location of school, date of graduation, or expected graduations
Major: Title of your major studies

Example:
Purdue University, West Lafayette, IN, Graduated 2020
Major: Aerospace Engineering

Version 2:
Name of degree, name of school. location of school. date of graduation or expected graduation.
Major: Title of your Major studies

Example:
Bachelor of Science, Purdue University, West Lafayette, IN, Graduated 2020
Major: Aerospace Engineering

Version 3:
Name of school. location of school. date of graduation or expected graduation.
Name of Degree, Title of Major

Example:

Purdue University, West Lafayette, IN, Graduated 2020

Bachelor of Science, Aerospace Engineering

Experience section:

Formatting your work experiences needs to fit the resume type you want to use.

Chronological, Combined, and Targeted resumes will usually list the name of the company first, location, dates employed, and then state the title of the job.

Functional resumes usually list the job title or skill under experiences and then late offer a list of employers using the name of company, location, and date.

But you can set up this section to what meets the needs of the application or position. Here are some examples of ways to write and set up your experience section.

Version 1:

Name of company, location of the company, and start date to end date or present.

- Title of Job

- Description of certain areas of the job

- Match the description of what you did on the job with the keywords from the future job description you want to apply

Example:

US Navy, NAS Fort Worth, 2016-2020

Title: Chaplain

- Provided religious ministry and support to service members and their families

- Facilitated religious ceremonies and services

- Cared for service members through the hospital and hospice areas

- Advised command on the right to exercise religious duties

Version 2:

Title of job, name of the company, and years worked

- Description of work duties

- Match the description of what you did on the job with the keywords from the future job description you want to apply

Example:

Chaplain, US Navy,   2016-2020

- Provided religious ministry and support to service members and their families
- Facilitated religious ceremonies and services
- Cared for service members through the hospital and hospice areas
- Advised command on the right to exercise religious duties

Version 3:

Name of company, the title of the job, and years served

- Description of work duties
- Match the description of what you did on the job with the keywords from the future job description you want to apply

Example:

US Navy, Chaplain,   2016–2020

- Provided religious ministry and support to service members and their families
- Facilitated religious ceremonies and services
- Cared for service members through the hospital and hospice areas
- Advised command on the right to exercise religious duties

Service years:

Years of service listed on a resume will give your age away. If you are concerned that age or your experience is making you overqualified for the position, then listing partial experience is often considered when developing the resume. I have often debated with my peers on this issue. Some of my older career counselors will tell the service member to leave off the years of service. This advice often brings sadness to some veterans because they are very proud of their service. My advice is to be proud and post it on your resume. Each day you served, you gained valuable work experience, training, and connections that you should be proud of.

Examples of how to list service under Work Experience or Employment Experience on a resume:

Example 1 (entire length and then each MOS description would break down the years working in that field:

United States Army, achieved the rank of Master Sergeant   1990–2008

(Then list each MOS from present to first, their job title, location, and years in that occupation)

Example 2: (If the company is not military-friendly, you can officially add the DOD as your employer since you do work in their division under the Armed services. And you follow command which comes from the Joint Chief of Staff who led the decisions of your branch for the government and DOD.)

Department of Defense, US Marine Corps.   2010–2021

Start Present MOS title, location of service, and year in MOS

Action Verb

Using verbs to start the description of your abilities in the experience section is important. Doing this helps define the skills and abilities you will offer to a company. The University of Wisconsin at Milwaukee's Career Development Center has a great Action Verb list that I often recommend to students at https://wm.edu/careerplan/wp-content/uploads/sites/73/2014/01/Tipsheet-Action-Verbs-Tan-1.pdf

Example of some action verbs you could use:

Assessed	Intervened
Coached	Mediated
Collaborated	Mobilized
Contributed	Moderated
Cooperated	Motivated
Demonstrated	Negotiated
Enabled	Provided
Encouraged	Referred
Ensured	Represented
Expedited	Resolved
Facilitated	Simplified
Focused	Supplied
Guided	Supported
Initiated	

Skills/Training

Most hard skills and a variety of soft skills can be listed by bullet link in this section. See Chapter Five for more information on your soft skills for this section of resume writing.

Some of the top skills looked for on resumes:

- "People" or Interpersonal Skills.
- Analysis or Critical Thinking.
- Problem-Solving/Solution Finder/Troubleshooter.
- Public Speaking/Communication Specialist.

- Customer Service Skills.

- Social Media Communication

- Collaborator/Team Work.

- Financial, Business or Accounting skills

- Counseling/Meditation/Coaching/Active Listener

- Adaptability/Flexible.

- Negotiation/Persuasion.

- Conflict Resolution/De-Escalation Specialist.

- Decision-making/Decisive leadership

- Empathy/Compassionate/Caring

- Management/Leader

- Organizational Specialist/Coordinator/Program Manager.

- Bilingual

- Administration/Coordinator/Project Management

- Time Management

- Computer Skills/Microsoft Proficient/Programing/Coding.

Master Resume

Let us begin with the MASTER RESUME set up:

The Master Resume will consist of every employment, occupation, educational and training certification or degrees, volunteer opportunities, Skills, and References you want to use in future targeted keyword resumes.

YOU DO NOT SEND THE MASTER RESUME TO EMPLOYERS

Set it up with every piece of history you have. This resume will be the resume you will gleam your information from to make your targeted resumes for jobs. This resume could be ten pages long or longer…this is where you will store all your professional employment history. Every certification, deployment, MOS, and job duties, experiences, and training. You will list locations, dates, supervisors, and duties for each work experience. For education, every credit, list some classes and GPA.

Benefits to creating a Master Resume that is fully written: Gleaming from the information you gathered, you can pick or choose what will benefit your job application by creating a two-page resume from the various parts of the Master resume's employment history.

Sections in your Master Resume:

HEADING
PROFESSIONAL SUMMARY
EDUCATION
WORK EXPERIENCE
SKILLS
VOLUNTEERING
AWARDS/ACCOMPLISHMENTS
REFERENCES

The following section will deal with the major differences between the ATS resume and a Job Fair resume.

Applicant Tracking System Resume

In the late 1990s, companies started using computer software that could filter resumes by keywords for a specific job. Today, almost all large companies use an applicant tracking system (ATS) to sort their resumes and filter by keywords. If the resume is not formatted correctly or written using the keywords found in the job description, the resume will be rejected. It is estimated that 75 percent of resumes are rejected by a computer before ever making it to a manager's desk.

The essential job of the ATS is to scan the resume based on a series of categories and specific keywords designed by the manager to filter out applicants. Today, there are over a dozen different ATS software options for employers to use. Each ATS filters or scans the code found in your downloaded resume differently.

The following ATS software is currently used (2021) by companies:

Oracle TALEO	Bamboo HR
BullHorn	UltiPro
Greenhouse Software	Silkroad
Homegrown iCims	CareerBuilder
Jobvite	Oracle
SAP Success	PeopleFluent
IBM Kenexa BrassRing	Cornerstone OnDemand
Workday	Symphony Talent
SAP SuccessFactors	NewtonSoftware
ADP	BreezyHR
SmartRecruiters	Workable
Lever	

Each of these programs will scan submitted resumes and filter them based on the criteria established by the hiring manager. A report will be created and sent to the hiring manager ranking the candidates based on the categories. Most hiring managers will only contact the top few names on the list for an interview.

To compete in this format, your resume will have to follow certain guidelines.

1. **Document identification:**

   When saving your resume make sure you are using Microsoft Word format (.doc). If you do not have Word then save your document as a .txt or .rtf format.

   Do not use .docx format in Word or .pdf, .html, .jpg or Open Office formats. Never send your resume as an image because it will not be read. PDF documents are often scanned in broken parts missing key information and fail to convert on the hiring managers system.

   Always save your resume with your first and last name in the title.

2. **Resume format**

   Arial is the best font to use for ATS coding. Times New Roman, Verdana, Georgia, and Garamond are other options but do not use Calibri or Cambria. Never use italics, underlines, or emojis.

   The size of the font should be between 10–12 and everything should be left aligned. The only item that can be center is the heading.

   Only use black ink and do not have images, pictures, shapes, or lines added to the resume. These items will stop the coding and prevent scanning by many ATS programs.

   One uses one-column resumes. Do not add tables, two columns, or graphs, they will stop the ATS coding from scanning your resume.

3. **Name and dates format**

   Make sure your full name is present at the top of the resume. The scan will label the report with your name since it will be the first code they translate.

   Do not use special characters, extra spaces, or generic nicknames. The system will be matching your resume code name with the name you applied to the online system.

   Always write the full year. Your dates should follow the format of MM/DD/YYYY or use just the year. Never use /, -, or ' characters to represent the year. Examples of what not to use: 03/20, 3-20, March '20.

4. **Border, bullets, and footers**

   Most borders and lines will stop the scan and reject a resume. It is best to leave them off of your resume.

   Do not use headers, footers, graphs, charts, logos, italics, and underlines.

   Bullets can be used if they are a circle and are not touching any text

Bold and caps can be used but not on the entire paper. Human eyes will see this paper eventually, so make it appealing but follow the guidelines.

Job Fair Resume

The benefits of a job fair resume are that you can be creative with the format. You can add color, graphics, different paper material, and you can add columns and keep it to one-page. Some companies prefer to look at a one-page resume for an initial meeting at a job fair. They may ask you to email them a detailed resume later.

Never add a photo to your resume but include a LinkedIn URL so they can look at your profile.

The biggest advantage to your resume for a job fair is to have multiple varieties of your resume.

Have a few one-page resumes that highlight your strengths, experiences, and skills. If your military experience is offering a few different career paths, make a few resumes that focus the skills on each path.

Do your research on the companies to be featured at the job fair. Usually, job fairs, such as the ones that recruitmilitary.com post at https://success.recruitmilitary.com/events, will post their sponsors and the companies hiring. They will also list specific jobs they are currently hiring for. By researching what is being offered, you can tailor a few resumes to meet those specific jobs.

Most recruiters will only have 30 seconds or less to look at your resume, so keep it clean and easy to read. Allow the eyes to lead to the specific skills and focus you want to showcase for these employers. Make sure you can talk about anything listed on your resume, the recruiters will ask for clarification on certain skills or employment history.

Always ask the recruiter or HR manager at the job fair for their business card. Send them your two-page resume with a nice thank you letter that addressed what you discussed with them at the job fair. And thank them for their time. Let them know how to contact you if they need any more information or have questions for you.

NINTH MONTH:
COVER LETTER AND REFERENCES

Month: _____

SUNDAY	MONDAY	TUESDAY	WEDNESDAY	THURSDAY	FRIDAY	SATURDAY

The objectives for Chapter Nine

- To understand the reason for a cover letter and how to develop one

- To understand the benefits of formatting the cover letter

- To develop and acquire references

- To format a reference page for an employment application

What is a Cover Letter and Why Do I Need One?

A cover letter is a candidate's introduction. The letter should unveil your personality by the way you discuss your qualifications and experiences. This letter allows the employers to see some of your soft skills and lets them know you can articulate/communicate. Also, the letter showcases your motivation and attitude toward this company and the position you are applying for.

Employers often view the cover letter as a way to see if the candidate will fit into the company culture based on the cover letter's explanation of their accomplishments, goals, and experiences. The biggest advantage of the cover letter is it can provide a connection between the candidate's career endeavors and the company's mission and values.

Cover letters should look like professional letters. The sections included in the letter are:

Heading

Date

Company Address

Greeting {Name of the HR manager or official}

Introduction

Body: {2 to 3 paragraphs that showcase all the reasons why you are qualified for this position. In this section, you will need to list your goals, employment endeavors, and how they connect to the company's mission/values, your accomplishments that match what they are looking for. Be specific, use numbers, data, and budget information.}

Conclusion: {Thank them for their time to review your qualifications and reiterate why you are the best person for this position. And end with the knowledge that they can contact you for additional information or an interview by leaving your contact information such as a phone or email or both.}

Ending plus Signature

Cover Letter Examples

{NAME}

{ADDRESS}

{PHONE NUMBER}

{EMAIL}

{LINKEDIN URL}

{DATE}

{COMPANY NAME}

{COMPANY ADDRESS}

{NAME OF THE HR MANAGER IF KNOWN} or {To Whom It May Concern}

I find the position advertised on the _____ {company site} _____ a great fit for my professional civilian career. I feel that I am well suited for this position and I would like to present my credentials for your consideration.

My work experience consists with over _____{years of (Add key words from the job description that match your skills: such as career communication, community relations, marketing, education, counseling, and career advising} experiences. I am currently a _{title}_____for the Department of Defense and the _____{branch of military such as United States Navy}where I _{job description}_____ throughout domestic and international Military installations and I am also a full time student at {name school}_____ where I am studying_{major}_____.

In the past my Military Occupations have consisted of the following duties _____{list jobs skills}_____ where I had to __{given specifics like worked with 3,000 employees to complete a project valued over $2.6 million}. I have been a {title}__ for_{branch}_____ and worked with various departments both civilian and federal.

My background consists of working with _{military, civilians, FEMA, government agencies—whoever fits the category}. I have worked with various local and national agencies. I have also worked with diverse groups in civilian and military industries and individuals for _{projects}__on a variety of situations.

I am seeking a chance to use my education, experiences, and military service to work for our government. I want to continue to work with federal, local, and community groups.

With Regards,

(NAME)

(Phone Number)

Another example of a Cover letter

{NAME}

{ADDRESS}

{PHONE NUMBER}

{EMAIL}

{LINKEDIN URL}

{DATE}

{COMPANY NAME}

{COMPANY ADDRESS}

{NAME OF THE HR MANAGER IF KNOWN} or {To Whom It May Concern}

I am writing to submit my resume for the {list job title} with {company name} at the {location} offices. I would like to present my credentials for consideration.

I have {years} experiences working with {list the job duty} for {branch or company}. I have excelled in this occupation through {list some of your accomplishments like managed a $3.2 million project, moved 400 tons of equipment internationally, organized and coordinated a battalion for deployment}. I plan to apply these skills, education, and experiences in my civilian career.

I find the position {name the job} at {name the company} to be a great fit for my career goals. I respect the {company's name} mission of {repeat the main mission} and believe I would be a great fit to participate in your workplace community. I plan to contribute to the {field of interest} and believe that {company's name} can provide me with this opportunity. I hope to apply my experiences in {name field} and become a valuable resource for {Company}

Thank you for taking the time to review my credentials for this position. If you would need further information or references, please contact me at {phone} or {email}. I look forward to further discussions about this position and your company.

{CLOSING REMARK}

{NAME}

{CONTACT INFORMATION including email}

Types of References

Who not to use as a reference?

Family: They know too much about you.

Domestic partners: They also know too much about you

Best friend/buddies: They can reveal too much about you

Neighbors: Sometimes they do not know you well enough

Questions to ask yourself about the references you have chosen

1. Is this person familiar with my work and would they make a positive statement about my work ethic?

2. Does this person have the time in their schedule to give me a reference whether by phone, email, or in person?

3. Does the person know of my current employment, experience, and life?

4. Is the person supportive of my endeavors?

5. Does the person have a good standing or reputation at the current company, business, or school?

If you have said NO to any of the above questions, do not despair. Many of these items can be fixed. If the person is not aware of your current work, then send them an update of your current work in the field, along with your accomplishments, and get them up to speed on your current situation. Send them a current resume so they can see what you did at the employment and your experiences. Create an open dialogue with the person so they will want to be supportive.

Research the candidate through company news, social media, and news outlets to make sure they can be a good reference.

When Gathering References

1. Ask their permission, every time, before adding or sending your person's name to a company as a reference.

2. Make sure the people give you current phone numbers and email addresses to use.

3. Send the job description and your current resume to each of your references to keep them informed of your job search.

4. Contact them after sending their reference into a job application to let them know they may be contacted for a reference

5. Maintain contact with them

6. Send them a thank you email after the reference given and let them know how grateful you are for their support

7. Contact them after finding out about the offer or denial to let them know what happened.

Reference Requests

Reference letters are usually written by employers, managers, educators, and customer businesses and can be given to you to use for any reference. They are usually more about your character and work ethic than about specific projects or skills.

The letter is similar to a recommendation letter where it will describe the person's character, qualification, training, and skillset. They often focus on the candidate and their work ethic while at employment or school. You can request a letter if you feel the person does not have the time to talk to an HR recruiter.

Always send a request for a reference referral or recommendation letter for every job you apply to and do this before you submit any person's name and contact information to a potential employer. Along with your request, send a copy of your resume and the job description. Also, send some information on the company you plan on applying to—this includes the address and phone number. Sometimes the references do not answer unknown phone numbers or emails, so when you send them the contact information, they will be aware of the area code or email id for the company in question.

Example for Military Reference Requests by Email

Dear {References full name, title}

My name is {Your name and title} and I served with you {the location and dates} in the {Division, battalion or regiment id}. I am writing to you because I am separating from the {Branch of military} in {month and year}and would be honored if you could provide me with a reference for my future civilian career applications. I believe you are the best qualified {title} to back up my qualifications and experience while serving in the {Branch of military}. I would sincerely be grateful for this reference.

Attached to this email for your review is my current resume and job description(s) that I will be applying to this week. I believe a positive reference from you regarding my qualification would benefit my chances of obtaining this job {or one of these positions}.

The company is called {name of company} and they are located at {location of company}. Their number is {phone number} and they specialize in {product or service}. If there is any further information you would need, please let me know at {your cell number}.

Thank you for your support for my transition,

{Full Name}

{contact information including email}

Example for Non-Military Reference Requests by Email

Dear {name of reference}

I am reaching out to request the ability to submit your name and contact information for a position as a {name the position} with {name the company}. Based on our years of working together, I believe you are the best person to discuss my professional work ethic and experiences with the hiring managers at {name the company}. I am confident that you will speak about my performance at {name your past employer} and my ability to work efficiently and diligently with you as my {job title of reference}. I am hoping that you can provide this information for this opportunity.

Attached you will find the job description, my resume, and the contact information for the company. If you require any other information, please do not hesitate to contact me at {cell phone number} or at {email}.

Thank you for your time and support of this endeavor,

Sincerely,

{name}

{contact information including email}

Reference Document

Scenario: The employer has now asked you to provide a reference document of three contacts that they can call about your credentials and work experiences.

You will create the Reference document using the same HEADING from your resume.

In this paper, you will list the Three References (two professional and one personal) or (all three professional) with the following information: full name of the person, their title and place of employment, their phone number, and email (ask them what number and email to use, most will give their cell phone number and email over their employment ones).

You should use at least two professional references for the document.

Professional: Manager, NCO, CO, or any leader that has known knowledge of your work ethic, experience, and skill set. Current and past co-workers with great work credentials that can verify your skills.

You should always have at least three professional references available for your job applications.

Three Professional References

Reference #1

Name: _____

Job Title: _____

Company: _____

Work Phone: _____

Cell Phone: _____

Work Email: _____

Personal Email: _____

LinkedIn url: _____

Reference #2

Name: _____

Job Title: _____

Company: _____

Work Phone: _____

Cell Phone: _____

Work Email: _____

Personal Email: _____

LinkedIn url: _____

Reference #3

Name: _____

Job Title: _____

Company: _____

Work Phone: _____

Cell Phone: _____

Work Email: _____

Personal Email: _____

LinkedIn url: _____

Personal References: Religious ministers, rabbis, leaders of your religion, professors/teachers/trainers, volunteer organizations, directors of organizations, coaches, customers, vendors, and mentors.

Three Personal References

Reference #1

Name: _____

Job Title: _____

Company: _____

Work Phone: _____

Cell Phone: _____

Work Email: _____

Personal Email: _____

LinkedIn url: _____

Reference #2

Name: _____

Job Title: _____

Company: _____

Work Phone: _____

Cell Phone: _____

Work Email: _____

Personal Email: _____

LinkedIn url: _____

Reference #3

Name: _____

Job Title: _____

Company: _____

Work Phone: _____

Cell Phone: _____

Work Email: _____

Personal Email: _____

LinkedIn url: _____

Template of a reference document to submit to employers:

{Your name}

{Address}

{phone}

{date}

{Company name}

{Address}

References for {Your name}

1. {Name of reference}

    {Title }

    {Name of company or branch of military}

    {Phone Number}

    {email}

    {Linkedin url}

2. {Name of reference}

    {Title }

    {Name of company or branch of military}

    {Phone Number}

    {email}

    {LinkedIn url}

3. {Name of reference}

    {Title }

    {Name of company or branch of military}

    {Phone Number}

    {email}

    {LinkedIn url}

Remember to only give them the number of references they requested. If they could not reach one of your references, they will contact you again for another one to replace the one they could not reach. This will allow you to know if you are still being considered for the position.

Reference Thank You

After knowing that the request was granted by your reference person and that they were contacted by the HR of your future employer, you should send a thank you email, note, or letter to your reference.

Example of a Thank You Letter

Dear {name of reference}

I just wanted to thank you for your acceptance and support by being a reference for me during my civilian job application phase. Transitioning from the military and obtaining a civilian career is a very challenging procedure and I am honored you agreed to assist me in this new endeavor. I will communicate with you about the further steps in this hiring process. And I will make sure you know if I have been offered a position with {name the company}. Your support during this process is appreciated.

Respectfully,

{name}

{contact info}

Keep the lines of communication open with your references when applying for civilian careers. Always approach the reference requirements with respect and appreciation. The easier you make this for your reference people and your future employer, the easier the hiring process becomes.

Let us check in with your decision:

My Decision on transition is to

_____

Confidence Meter: How Confident are you with your decision?

$$1 - 2 - 3 - 4 - 5 - 6 - 7 - 8 - 9 - 10$$

Unsure   Almost sure   Very Sure

Remember this decision is not a reality until you receive your DD-214. If you decide to wait and stay in the military, then tuck this book away until you are ready to transition. If you want to continue, head-on to the next chapter

TENTH MONTH:

JOB HUNTING 101

Month: _____

SUNDAY	MONDAY	TUESDAY	WEDNESDAY	THURSDAY	FRIDAY	SATURDAY

The objectives for Chapter Ten

- To understand the methods and guidelines for job searching

- To learn the history behind the modern version of job searches

- To understand the importance of networking to gain employment

- To learn about the different job search tools available for veterans.

Job search skills have changed drastically in the last 20 years. Gone are the days of seeking a job through local pin board advertisements, newspapers, or dropping off your resume at a business.

If your area still has a published newspaper, you will find very limited options and access to job opportunities in the Help Wanted Ads posted in the Classified section. The modern practice of searching for employment requires knowledge of a computer and the Internet's social media.

Modern Job Hunting 101

In the 1990s, the dawn of the Internet age, job search engines were created. Websites such as Monster, CareerBuilder, and HotJobs were the top contenders for job searches. The avenue in which they acquired jobs to post required selling space on their website to employers. The employers than would advertise their openings.

In 1998 the first Applicant Tracking Systems were created which made using the internet beneficial to employers for their job openings. This new hiring system would process resumes, filtering them based on keywords for the HR Managers. This was a game-changer for hiring.

In 2003, LinkedIn was launched and it changed how online job searches were conducted because it allowed candidates to search HR Managers for a company, reach out to them and look at the openings for the employers while also researching about the company's history. The biggest benefit of LinkedIn was the communication and networking ability. LinkedIn today is even more advanced. With the multiple members, opportunities, and networks, a job candidate could easily access resources, people working in the same field, same company and gain valuable knowledge to use during the interview process such as company data, history, and information.

To learn more on how to access LinkedIn for veterans and get a discount on their membership go to Military & Veterans | Social Impact (linkedin.com) at https://socialimpact.linkedin.com/programs/veterans.

Most TAP programs give transitioning members a brief explanation on how to use LinkedIn for networking.

The famous Indeed.com was developed in 2004 and it was followed by various job site options such as Snagajob. Indeed has grown since its inception and today is the number one job search engine. Most job seekers will have the Indeed app on their smartphone.

By 2007, virtual and remote jobs were opening to the public. FlexJobs will be one of the first "work at home" job search sites. The same year that FlexJobs was launched, the National Labor-Exchange created an electronic labor-exchange network that worked with the NASWA and the Direct Employers Association, and their site to search for jobs is found at usnlx.com. Today, the National Labor-Exchange has created a database of virtual jobs to search at virtualjobs.usnlx.com

2008 introduced the famous salary and job search engine known as Glassdoor. By 2010, multiple other search engines and "ZipRecruiter" sites emerged. In 2013, the Online Apply button was created for Monster to allow the candidate the ability to apply to jobs directly on the job search engine. In 2021, the job search engines created almost 30 years ago are still active and popular.

Searching the Internet for Employment Opportunities

1. 1. Not all job titles for a specific career are the same. Before using a job search engine go back to the O*Net site and look up all the variations available for occupation.

   Go to www.onetonline.org/find/ and enter your job title of interest and then use all the different variations of this job scope to search in the job search engines.

   Example:

   In O*Net put in the **keyword section**: Aviation Mechanic.

   A list of different occupations will appear.

   Click on the first one: Aviation Mechanic and Service Technician

   On the **Summary Report** for Aviation Mechanic and Service Technician you will see a section called:

   Sample of reported job titles.

   In that section you will see the following titles:

   Aircraft Maintenance Technician (Aircraft Maintenance Tech),

   Aircraft Mechanic,

   Aircraft Restorer,

   Aircraft Technician,

   Airframe and Powerplant Mechanic (A & P Mechanic),

   Aviation Maintenance Technician (AMT),

   Aviation Mechanic,

   Helicopter Mechanic

   Now go to **Indeed.com** and pick one of these job titles to search. I strongly suggest looking through all the variations of this job scope and its multiple titles to see what alternative titles appear.

2. The jobs posted in the Job Search Engines may not be available. As you know from previous readings in this chapter, job search engines make their money from sharing their space with employers. If a job was

filled, the job search website is not going to know unless the recruiter or HR manager contacts them to take the job down. Some HR managers may keep the job up to glean resumes for future positions. The job posting usually has a prepaid time limit and regardless if the job was filled, the job will be visible until the time limit expires.

So to know if a job posted on Monster or Indeed is still available, go to the company's career page and see if it is posted. Also, you can use LinkedIn to reach out to an HR manager about the job.

3. Always apply to the company's website and not through the job search engines. Remember the job search engine website is also a filtering system or ATS for the company. Take the effort and apply it directly to the company. Give your resume a better chance to be seen by the HR manager.

Networking 101

The fastest way to land a job is through networking. Back in the early days of the Industrial Revolution, employers would bring whole families over to work in the factories. The idea of one good worker would know more good workers was essential for the factory floor and to production. That concept is still treasured by employers today. Many companies have a referral plan to encourage employees to refer people for open positions.

Employment Networking

- **Family**: Many transitioning veterans return to their hometowns after years of service. Some family members may help and network for them to create job opportunities. I often suggest transitioning service members reach out to the family for options in their hometown.

- **Friends**: Whether you went to school with these people, served in the military with them, or met them at the gym, friends can often suggest, hint, and even refer transitioning military personnel for careers in the civilian world. Lockheed Martin is famous for having referrals from veteran employees of battle buddies for open positions.

- **Teachers/Trainers/Mentors:** It is a great idea for veterans wanting to work in the school districts to network with past teachers or with trainers at companies they have worked within the military. I often see veterans move into trainer positions with companies whose products they used while serving. They would network with the trainers who taught them to successfully use the equipment.

- **Community/Places of Worship/Organizations:** Reaching out to various groups of people about seeking a civilian career is an excellent way to find one. Mentioning to neighbors or peers that you have decided to leave the service and would love to find a job in the area is a great way to network. People love to help and be of service. You just have to ask. Churches can have members that are CEOs, HR managers, and know of open positions. Organizations often will hold job fairs and have contacts with area companies. As you get closer to separating you will need to put yourself out in the public to get noticed and find network groups to help.

- **Military organizations, non-profits, and groups:** They often hold job fairs, "meet and greets" and zoom sessions for networking with transitioning service members and veterans.

Some of the biggest networking sites to use are listed here:

- Recruitmilitary.com hosts job fairs across the nation and they also list jobs.
- Military.com Mentor Network has many ways to help veterans including a career center
- RallyPoint.com is a social network that helps with job placement
- HireaHero.org offers many career options including zoom networking sessions
- VetFriends.com has multiple communities and events
- Veterati.com offers mentorship and networking and is people-focused
- Vet2industry.com is a free resource library of resources to help veterans

Finding Job Leads

- **At work:** Next time you head into your military job, look around at the equipment you use or the contractors you work with and see what companies are listed on those devices, work orders, or that you deal with daily. These are leads. Research those companies, find out who is the contact for them for your division or base. Connect with them on LinkedIn and send them a note telling them you have worked with their devices or equipment for many years and would love to work for their company after your service is complete.

    Example: Signaling Officer for US Army uses Man Tech equipment and contractors.

    Reaches out through contractors to find out about transitioning to this company.

    The company at www.mantech.com/careers/transitioning-military offers multi-positions. The service member looks at the SkillBridge option to work before terminating.

- **In your city/town or location:** Regardless of where you will live after separating, take time to research that location. Try to visit the location and drive around to see the industry, the corporations, and the opportunities. Sometimes if you go to a Chamber of Commerce in a city, they will have a booklet with the listing of the business in the region and their website could discuss the same information. Use LinkedIn to search out current opportunities in the area and research job trends using O*Net.

- **Hobbies and passions**: If your passion is hunting and you want to seek out jobs that allow you to hunt, look at careers in the places that you can partake in this activity, such as game wardens, hunting equipment manufacturing, hunting supply stores, gun ranges, etc.

If you love to work out and be physically fit seek out jobs in those categories. Places like 24-hour Fitness and Golds Gym offer programs to hire veterans for management-level jobs and they pay well. If you love your Air Jordans and would love to be able to work in this industry look at places that sell this product or look at the manufacturer.

Think outside of the box when seeking employment. Sometimes the best opportunities are ones we make for ourselves.

My Decision on transition is to

_____

Confidence Meter: How Confident are you with your decision?

$$1 - 2 — 3 — 4 — 5 — 6 — 7 — 8 — 9 — 10$$

Unsure   Almost sure   Very Sure

Remember this decision is not a reality until you receive your DD-214. If you decide to wait and stay in the military, then tuck this book away until you are ready to transition. If you want to continue, head-on to the next chapter

ELEVENTH MONTH:

INTERVIEW TRAINING

Month: _____

SUNDAY	MONDAY	TUESDAY	WEDNESDAY	THURSDAY	FRIDAY	SATURDAY

The objectives for Chapter Eleven

- To understand the interview process
- To learn about the interview formats and understand what is expected with each format
- To understand how to prepare for an interview

Interview Formats

Depending on the industry and the focus of the job, interviews can be conducted in a variety of ways.

- **Traditional interviews**

  Face to face with one or more managers asking the candidate a series of questions about the job, the experience, work ethic, and company knowledge.

- **Committee/Panel interviews**

  A series of interviews where the candidate will be asked questions by a panel of managers, supervisors, and HR representatives. The Military tends to use these methods of panel-style questioning.

- **Group interviews/interactions**

  A small to a large group of candidates placed in a situation with a task, or a group gathering to observe interactions, cooperation, and teamwork. This interview style usually has an objective to complete, typically within a time limit. Observing for leadership skills and collaboration are the main reason for conducting this type of interview.

- **Presentation interviews**

  A gathering of applicants to observe a presentation about the company, the job scope, and sometimes the challenges of the job. From this format, candidates can be called into a panel, group, or traditional interview.

- **Situational/Behavioral interviews**

  Scenario questions are usually the basis of this interview but in some cases, they may even put the candidate in a situation to see how they react or handle the event. The interviewers are looking at overall character and problem-solving abilities.

- **Virtual/Video conference interviews**

  Virtual interviews are usually two or more managers on a video call format where questions are asked. The candidate is also observed for their ability to handle technology, control their environment, and their ability to handle virtual presentations. Most remote job positions will have a video conference-style interview.

- **Coffee/Lunch meal interviews**

  The candidate is asked to meet at a public restaurant or location where food will be served. This type of interview is also observing you outside of the office or business setting. The goal is to ask you questions about your abilities while you are more relaxed. The interview is also to observe how you conduct yourself with those around you and in a public setting. In this interview, you will have to be mindful of what you order. Do not order food that is runny, saucy, or spicy. Avoid soups, salads, and spaghetti. Regardless of what the interviewer orders, stay away from alcoholic and carbonated beverages. Do not eat before the interviewer does and always taste your food first before adding condiments, salt, or pepper. This can be a behavioral type of interview.

- **Work example interview**

  The candidate is asked to demonstrate their skills or trade. The display or situation that needs to be fixed is in the room where the interviewers can observe the candidate's skill set. In this type of interview, the company should inform the candidate beforehand so the candidate can dress accordingly and bring essential tools. Always ask the person setting up the interview what kind of attire is expected for the interview and if you would need to bring steel-toed boots, safety glasses, tools, and hardware.

- **Peer group interview**

  This type of interview usually happens for interval hires when the candidate is moving to a new project or program. In this case, the candidate would be interviewed by the peers they will work with and among. The questions would be geared to knowledge base questions on the project, program, manufactured item, or software. Technology job interviews can involve peers who would work with the candidate if hired.

- **Telephone/Cell phone interview**

  The candidate would receive a call at a designated time to answer questions. The call could house more than one interviewer. Obstacles to this type of interview can include missing the call, not having the phone powered, limited connections, and interference. Never conduct the interview call while driving. Try to find a location that is quiet so you can be heard, and you can hear them. Try to conduct the call where there are limited distractions.

- **Stress interview**

  The interview involves uncomfortable and often situational or scenario type of questions. The interview is focused on how you react to the question, the situation, and if you can handle stress. Law enforcement, medical and sales jobs tend to ask these types of questions.

- **Selection interview**

  An in-depth questionnaire is given before being interviewed traditionally. Sometimes the interview is just answering a series of questions on the computer. Depending on the job, sometimes a traditional interview can follow these questionnaires.

- **Off-site interview**

  Larger companies will hold interviews at a convention center or a hotel. Knowledge about the company will be crucial for this type of interview because you will not see the actual company location. Research the company and be prepared to discuss what they do, how they are doing, and who their competitors are.

- **On-the-spot interview**

  Job fairs tend to have these types of interviews and if you hand-deliver your resume, you may experience this type of interview. Sometimes in the military, contractors will work with our service members and they may recommend your abilities to the company they work for, leading to an on-the-spot interview with a manager.

- **Structured interview**

  Same questions, the same format of questioning, and the same number of interviewers involved in this style of interview. The federal government and most state government employers conduct their interviews this way to meet the guidelines of the Equal Employment Opportunity Commission (EEOC).

Interview Stages

Screening Calls

Usually, to set up the interview, the candidate will receive a phone call from the Human Resource manager. This is the first introduction to the company. Make sure you ask this person some key questions. You may also receive an email with interview information, but you can still respond to ask questions.

Questions to ask if they have not informed you:

1. How many people will be interviewing me?

2. Attire for the interview—is business or casual attire preferred? What would you recommend for the interview? You can explain that you just spent many years wearing a uniform, so any help on dress attire to help you make a good impression would be appreciated.

3. Should I bring work clothes to incase they want to see my skillset (Steel-toed boots, protective gear, tools)

4. Is there parking near this location?

5. How long is the interview expected to be?

6. Do I need to bring any other information with me for this interview? (ID, certification, transcripts)

Preparing for the Day of the Interview

- **Location:** If you have never been to the location for the interview and you live in a large city or area, drive out to the location the day before at the same time of the interview. Know the drive and how much time you will need to get there.

- **Parking:** Find parking and allow yourself enough time to look over your resume, research, and job description. Plan to be at least 30 minutes early so you can ground yourself before going into the interview.

- **Observe the company:** Observe the people, the environment, and your reaction to what you see. This is your first impression of the company. Sometimes how you feel in a location can tell you if it is the right fit for you. Never ignore how you feel in a location.

- **Review the job description:** Re-read the job description and think of questions you would ask of someone interviewing for this job. Answer your questions.

- **Know the company:** Research their history and know their mission statement. Read their website, read reviews of their products, business, and people. Know the CEO and key leaders of the company. Know who their biggest competitors, clients, and customers are.

- **Communication:** Let family, friends, and anyone who needs to communicate with you know that you will be unreachable during the time of your interview. Cell phones should be left in the car or turned off during the interview so as not to distract. If you are waiting in a room before the interview, use this time to study the company, ask questions of the greeter/administrator, read the company's brochures, review your resume or job description materials or greet other candidates. The company can observe candidates even in the waiting room. Those who sit on their phones instead of interacting or learning more about the company can lose the advantage.

- **Other tips:** Use the restroom when you can. If you are nervous avoid drinking anything before the interview. Also do not chew gum or have anything chewy in your mouth before or during the interview. Also, if you smoke cigarettes, know the company's policy about tobacco products and avoid partaking in this activity before dressing for the interview. Make sure you have a pen and tablet of paper to write information down during the interview.

Attire for the Interview

Unless the company specifies what to wear, always dress in business attire. First impressions are visual and dressing professionally shows the employer you are confident and capable.

Three areas you are visually assessed involve clothes, hairstyle, and grooming.

If your job is trade or manufacturing, call ahead and ask HR if the attire is to work in a shop setting or dress to showcase the talents. If they say you will do both a formal interview and a skillset example, then dress business but bring your work clothes in a bag to change into. IF they say you would need to showcase your skill set in an interview, then you should wear a solid t-shirt, work pants, steel-toed boots, bring safety glasses and tools and make sure to remove all jewelry/metals in advance.

Attire Guidelines

1. Dark colors: Black, blue or gray (stay away from bold patterns or loud colors)

2. Coordinate the slacks with the jacket. Even if the slacks and the jacket have pockets, avoid putting your hands in them.

3. White, or solid color shirt. Wear an undershirt/tanktop if you need to cover tattoos or the shirt is thin.

4. Ties are needed for certain business suits. You can have a tie with a pattern if the shirt is a solid color. If the shirt has pinstripes, the tie will need to be a solid color.

5. For casual attire, plain solid colored polo/blouse with slacks that are black, blue, gray, or brown/khaki.

6. Belt color should match the shoe color.

7. Wear dark shoes with dark socks. Make sure the shoes are polished or in decent order. No loafers, flats, tennis shoes, or sneakers. If work boots are required, they must be regulation. Heels should be business medium style, no open-toed or heel.

8. Grooming: Shave, shower, clean and cut nails, wear deodorant, avoid heavy makeup, avoid strong cologne or perfume, brush teeth, avoid smoking and wear modest jewelry (simple earrings, one ring per hand, and one bracelet if necessary).

9. Until you know the environment of the company, cover tattoos and remove facial/body piercings for the interview.

10. Hair should be away from the eyes and mouth. Tied back or in a professional style.

11. Accessories should be minimal. Avoid wearing sunglasses, hats, excessive jewelry, or carrying oversized bags or multiple bags. Briefcases and bags should be a solid color that matches your attire: black, blue, gray, or beige.

12. Avoid oversized, tight, revealing, low cut, see-through clothes or clothes with messages/letters on them.

13. If you wear glasses, make sure they stay on your face. Clean your lenses.

14. If the company mandates masks to cover the nose and mouth, then you will need to make sure your mask follows those guidelines and matches your attire. Avoid any political, comical, or wordy masks. Stick with black or blue solid masks.

Interview Introductions

Formal initial impressions set the stage for the entire interview. Make sure you are fully present in this introduction. Stand up to greet the person calling your name.

Be aware of how the manager or interviewer introduces their name. If they go formal and introduce their name with a title (Dr., Mr., or Mrs.), remember to use this title throughout the interview. Also pay attention if they choose certain pronouns to identify, respectfully follow their lead in the introduction stage.

Due to the COVID-19 social guidelines instituted in 2020, most employers may avoid handshakes. Let them lead the interview, then if they do offer a gesture like a handshake, you can decide if you do want to participate.

Showcase a smile, even if wearing a mask, to show your enthusiasm for the interview and opportunities. If you are nervous and tend to sweat, make sure you carry a handkerchief to help the situation. If you tend to chuckle when you are nervous, you can let the interviewer know how excited you are to be given this opportunity.

Build a rapport by showing respect for the interviewer. Letting them lead the interview also means allowing them to sit first, talk first, and initiate the tone of the meeting.

Also stay away from small talk that involves discussing personal information, controversial subjects, and politics. Confidence can be projected while being quiet. The attitude of respect should be projected towards everyone at that company from the gatekeeper to the CEO.

Employer Questions

Most interview questions have a pattern. The questions will relate to the job or product, your resume and skill set, your work experience, and your ability to fit the job and company.

Examples of questions they may ask:

1. Tell me a little about yourself?

In this situation, be real. Talk about some adventures you have experienced, personal or job-related. In the Military, you could have jumped out of a plane, worked with nuclear items, visited Japan, and been deployed to the Middle East. Do not be vague or boring, tell something you are proud about or worked very hard for. Showcase something you are passionate about, something you achieved, or a time when you overcame a challenge. The employer is looking for a brief introduction, key accomplishments, key strengths, and goals.

2. Tell me about a difficult problem you faced at work and explain how you dealt with it?

Make sure you discuss a real problem you faced in your career that involved a solution. Most people when they solve a situation at work, whether it was a project, a deadline, a transportation issue, an operation/mission, or a broken product, can tell you exactly what they went through to fix it, solve it or complete it. They can also discuss how they troubleshoot the situation or product just to complete the mission and if they could have had more time or resources, how they would have done it differently. In this case, the answer is detailed and showcases truth and facts. Remember some of the experience in the military cannot be discussed due to clearance issues, so think of situations that you can discuss before your interview.

3. What does "failure" mean to you?

The question makes the candidate remember how they overcame obstacles. The interviewer is looking for honesty about bad choices or decisions and how the candidate learned from this situation. Accepting fault is about understanding where to improve. The resiliency or determination to improve is a character trait this question is trying to display.

4. How would your co-workers describe you?

This question is looking for character traits by asking you to describe what another would say about you. Be cautious with this answer and describe a person who would be a great fit for the job by discussing their skills.

5. What do you know about our company?

Your previous research will allow you to discuss who they are, what they did when they were created, and how they are doing.

6. What interested you the most about this job?

Using your research of the company, the product, and the services, you will be able to discuss how the company is a great fit for your experiences and skills. You can discuss any previous experience you had with their products or their company and why you want to work with this company.

7. Explain your qualifications for this job?

This question allows you to tie in your skillset with the keywords from the job description. Pick more than two skills or experiences to discuss that match the job description.

Key Tips

- Always try to match your skills with the keywords in the job description when discussing your talent or the job.

- Keep your answer brief but to the point. Try not to talk too much, rattle on, or go off-topic when answering questions.

- Do not volunteer information, discuss personal, religious, or political history.

- Think before you speak and take the time to formulate your answer. It is acceptable to pause before answering. Be active in your listening. Do not interrupt and repeat the question or ask for clarification of the question if you are concerned about how to answer. Speak clearly and not too fast or loudly. Communication skills will be assessed in the interview.

- Make eye contact and smile while answering the questions. Keep your hands in your lap and try not to fidget in your seat. If you bring a paper and a pen, then write, scribble or make scratch marks to let go of nervous tension.

- Be mindful and fully present at the moment. Try not to become despondent. Be enthusiastic and encouraging in your energy.

- Watch your tone of voice and manners. Sometimes the interviewer may be a college intern or unskilled/ inexperienced. A presentation by an inexperienced person may cause frustration or tension, do not let it show. Roll with it, see it as an adventure, and try to make the inexperienced interviewer relaxed and comfortable. Defuse the situation and ground yourself into a stable and calm demeanor.

- Do not exaggerate and do not boast in your answers. Avoid negative storytelling or associations. Do not appear desperate or needy, focus on how interested you are in the position and the company.

Items of Concern

Under the EEOC and the Fair Employment Practices Commission guidelines, no employer is allowed to ask a candidate about their demographics. If in an interview, these guidelines and policies are ignored, and a question about your gender, sexuality orientation, family or family label, nationality, race, religion, health status, or age is asked, you can simply answer:

"I do not plan on discussing this subject in an interview. I would prefer to continue discussing my skill sets and experiences pertaining to this job."

For some military, sometimes the interviewer may have also had military experiences and will sometimes ask off-topic questions and about the military. Under no condition should any veteran have to discuss any combat-related experiences or any health-related experiences/treatments in a job interview. Always be mindful that the questions should be focused on the job and your skillset for the job.

"Thank you for asking about my service, I proudly served my country but now I want to proudly work for your company. So, what else can I tell you about my ability to do this job?"

Sign language interpreters, reading assistance, facility access, and on-site testing alternative formats are accommodations that should already be in place by the company. Ask about the hiring process, interview process, and what to expect in the next stages of this process. Do your research about the company, the position, and the work environment. Review the company's responsibilities under the Americans with Disabilities Act (ADA).

The company is legally prohibited from asking questions that could reveal a disability. Only after the candidates request accommodations can the company discuss the disability. The candidate should inform the HR department before the interview if any of these accommodations are needed to conduct the interview. Be specific in what you need for accommodations. The company may request a healthcare provider note to confirm the impairment and need for accommodations.

The interviewer should not ask about any health-related or disability concerns. But be prepared for a question related to concerns.

They can ask:

"Are there any concerns that you have about working the job scope or performing the duties required for the position?"

Candidate's Questions

Always have a couple of questions ready to ask them. Most interviewers usually end with "Do you have any questions or concerns you would like to discuss?"

It is important to show interest in and awareness of the company and interview. Some questions to ask:

1. Could you describe a typical day in this position or job? What can I expect of the job scope? Or What can I expect in the first 90 days of working in this position?

2. What other departments, positions, and people would I interface or interact with? Would I be a part of a team or group?

3. What training or educational opportunities does your company offer for this position?

4. What further education, skills, or training does the company encourage their employees to have? Based on my resume, what other skills or training would you recommend I obtain?

5. What is the next step in the interview process? How soon do you plan on filling the position? May I follow up with you about the position in the next week?

6. Is there any travel expected for this position? How does your company handle travel arrangements?

7. Is it possible to have a tour of the plant or see where the position is located?

8. During the COVID-19 pandemic, what safety measures did/does your company take to ensure the health and safety of your employees? And what is expected from your employees to guarantee this safety?

9. How does your company handle diversity and inclusion in the workplace? What supports are in place for diverse populations at this company?

10. Based on my resume and interview, how well did I compare to those you have already interviewed for this position? Where do I stack against the other candidates for the position?

Closing Stage

Thank everyone involved in your interview and let them know you are still interested by stating that you look forward to hearing from them soon. If they have business cards, ask for them. You will want to send each person a thank you email for spending the time with you. Some managers find personalized mailed thank you cards a better format. Sending one is what matters.

Example of a Thank You Message

Email: Address each person separately.

Mailed letter: Make sure you have your address first on the paper, their address next, the date, the title

Your Name,

Your street address

City, state, zip code

Date

Company name

Address

City, state, zip code

(Name of the person, their title)

Thank you for the opportunity to interview for the position of __(title of the job)_____ for __(name of the company)__. It was a pleasure meeting you and learning more about your company. I was interested in this position because……….(mention how your skills match or how you enjoy working in this field or with this company). If you need any additional information, verification of skills or to discuss further my abilities to successfully perform this job, please feel free to contact me at ____(Leave phone number).

I look forward to speaking with you again and I am encouraged by the possibility of joining your staff. Thank you again for the consideration.

Sincerely,

(Your full name).

As you exit the company or location, make sure you say goodbye or thank you to those people who interacted with you: including the administrator, the gatekeeper, if at a restaurant the waitress, and hostess. Smile and be personable as you leave.

Do not start taking off your attire or becoming casual before you get to your car. Do not take off ties or jackets until in your vehicle.

Once back in the car, on paper write down how you feel, what you experienced, and what concerns you may have. This will help you later in deciding if you want to take the position.

Job Fairs Quick Interview

I had mentioned a couple of chapters back that recruiters and hiring managers at job fairs may only have 30 seconds to talk with you about your resume. In that very short time frame, job seeker can sell their experiences and highlight their main points for being hired. It is a technique for pitching your skills and experience known as the 30-second elevator speech.

This speech is a very clear and brief message about what you can offer to the company. It is also used to introduce yourself and open a dialogue between you and the recruiter.

Before starting this technique, you will need to investigate what company you want to talk to at the job fair. And you will need to visit this company's website before going to the job fair to see what positions are currently open. Sometimes the company will interview for positions that will open in the following quarter. Researching the company, their current opportunities and they type of work they do will benefit you in a job fair environment.

The Technique

1. Write a speech in about 90 words that describes you, what you can offer a company as far as skills and experiences are concerned, and why you are a great candidate for the positions you found on their site. It is crucial to use keywords in your speech. Also tell them about you, what you have done, and explain why you are interested in this company. Include a specific example of your skill or experience. Conclude the speech by asking for a business card or feedback concerning your resume.

2. Practice this elevator speech and time it. IF it is over 30 seconds you will need to trim some of the excesses off of it. Practice saying it to another person and stand about 6 feet from them. Ask them to write down what they heard you say. Pay attention to what the person honed in on when they were listening to you. Did they hear what you wanted to stress about yourself and your experiences? If not, go back and clear the speech up.

3. Also pay attention to why items may have been missed, ask yourself if you were loud enough to be heard. You do not want to yell or seem like your screaming, but you want to be heard. At most of the veteran job fairs, there can be up to 25,000 people in a location. It can be very loud with multiple people talking around you.

4. Space and loudness at job fairs can create anxiety and stress. Prepare yourself to have your space invaded and multiple groups talking at once around you.

5. Be confident and proud of your skills and experience. Let your voice showcase this enthusiasm and confidence. Ask the person you are practicing with if you sound confident in your experiences.

6. Smile and make eye contact with the recruiter or hiring manager at the job fair. Unlike the rules of engagement in the military, eye contact is favored in the civilian world because it shows confidence and openness to communicate.

7. Be ready for questions on what you discussed in your 30-second speech and what you presented in the resume. Before attending the job fair, think of questions that may come up about what you will present.

Template for a 30-second speech

To prepare for a job fair quick interview, use the template on the next page to prepare what you would say and practice this interview template. This can also be used for cold-calls about jobs or emails to network.

	Your introduction:
1. Introduction: Introduce who you are and your current situation that brought you to the job fair **Starter sentence examples:** Hello, my name is Joanne Smith and I am wrapping up a 10-year career with the US Army. I would like to present my resume to be considered for open positions within your company. Hello, my name is John Hall and I will be retiring from the US Navy in the next month. I would like to present my credentials for the position of operations manager for your company.	

2. Highlight experience
 	
Discuss some specific skills, experiences, and accomplishments that highlight why you are the best candidate for this company or open position.
 	
Starter sentence examples:
 	
During my time in the Army,
 	
    I had to…..
 	
    I acquired the following skills…..
 	
    I developed some valuable experiences such as…..
 	
    I learned to….
 	
    I was taught….
 	
    I was provided opportunities to…..
 	
In my 20 plus years of service, I was given many opportunities to……
 	
Under notable leadership, I was able to ……
 	
During my military career, I experienced …..	

3. Skills

List 3 Skills: Soft or hard to showcase

Go back to Chapter Five to review what skills you found and pick three to discuss in this speech

Examples:

Organizational or coordinating skills

Project management

Leadership/Supervisory

Perceptual skills

4. **Plan or career goal**

Discuss what you are looking for or the opportunities you hope this company can give you.

Starter sentence examples:

I see that your company is currently hiring for ……….. and I feel that I am a perfect fit for this position.

I am interested in applying for ………

I have over 10 years of working with your product and I believe my experience would benefit your company.

I am seeking a position with your company because I ……

I would like to find a company that could utilize my work experience and training.

5. Closure/Ending

Always thank them for their time. Let them know you are available for interviews and ask them about the timeframe of the hiring process. Also, obtain their contact information.

Examples:

Thank you for taking the time to speak with me about your company. If possible, could I have your contact information so I could discuss further the opportunities at your company?

Thank you for allowing me to present my resume. I was wondering about the hiring process; do you know the timeline for hiring someone for this position?

Side notes:

Make sure you take something to write on with in case you have to take their information down or give information.

Take your smartphones to a job fair. Just make sure your phone is on silent during the discussion times with the recruiter. Using a smartphone to take photos of business cards can save you time. Some phones can download information and contact numbers. Some companies have QR codes (scannable squares) with company and contact information.

Now put this template together into one speech using the lined section below:

_____

_____

_____

_____

_____

_____

_____

_____

_____

_____

_____

_____

_____

_____

_____

_____

_____

_____

_____

_____

_____

_____

_____

_____

_____

_____

_____

_____

Time yourself: _____ seconds

Do you see any places you can trim off or add to?

TWELFTH MONTH:
SECURING THE CIVILIAN CAREER

Month: _____

SUNDAY	MONDAY	TUESDAY	WEDNESDAY	THURSDAY	FRIDAY	SATURDAY

The objectives for Chapter Twelve

- To understand the parts of an offer letter

- To learn how to write an offer acceptance letter

- To understand the importance of career negotiation

- To learn how to write a rejection or negotiation letter

Before we start this chapter, we need to clarify something:

Unless you have a written offer letter/email with the company's letterhead, a salary, and a start date listed, you do not have a job offer.

Many times, I have coached and consulted with transitioning service members who swore up and down that they had a verbal job offer and it would begin when they separated.

I would inquire on how they knew of this opportunity? They often confirmed with a story of a friend promising them a position at the company or they talked to a recruiter who claimed it was a done deal. And in believing this story, those transitioning members did nothing to prepare for their separation and future civilian career. Fast forward the first month of civilian life and they have no job, no resume prepared, and are very overwhelmed.

So be warned that a job is only guaranteed when the offer is given in a letter/email format and is listing important items such as salary, start date, vacation, and benefits. An offer letter allows you to negotiate or discuss the specifics of the position before you accept it.

In Chapters Two and Three, we looked at your finances and medical. You now understand what you will need to be successful and comfortable while living in the civilian world.

Components of an Offer Letter/Email

The basic components of your letter/email will first consist of the congratulations and welcome to the company paragraph which will list your official job title.

The next part of your letter or email is the job description and should list some of the expected duties and requirements of the job. If it is not listed in your offer letter, ask HR to send you a detailed job description before you sign the offer. Review the offer and make sure it is the job you applied and interviewed for. Keep this job description with you until you move to another position. At any time if the manager tries to alter or add to your job description, you can negotiate your salary and other package deals.

1. **Salary:** Monetary compensation for your work is the whole reason you are seeking employment. Sometimes the offer is in hourly wages and others are salary. Spend a while researching similar jobs in competitor companies to see what they are paying for the same job. Know what you are worth and what you need for a salary. Sometimes you can negotiate for more money but often you have to prove that you deserve more than what they are offering. Often it is easier to ask for more of the other items than it is for more pay.

2. **Benefits**: Medical, dental, life, accidental and vision insurances fall under this category. Research what healthcare or insurance providers the company offers and the costs of each of their plans. The majority of your deductions from your paycheck will be for insurance costs.

3. **Education assistance**: Find out if they offer to pay for further education, training, and certification. This could aid in your future endeavors.

4. **401K or pension plans**: Most employers offer a 401K instead of a pension. Find out the matching contributions and the limit amount you can invest while employed with this company.

5. **Stocks and equity options**: Ownership in a company is an amazing opportunity and many smaller companies offer this option.

6. **Profit sharing:** Discuss with the employer if they participate in profit sharing. Learn the company's rules of engagement in this benefit and their percentage offered. This benefit exists to help fuel productivity and retention.

7. **Allowances** for work-related items: Gas miles, work clothes, and supplies, travel and transportation costs (including train fare or vehicle leasing). Sometimes asking for a company vehicle or vouchers for the train can help cut your personal budget and allow for your money to be spent on other items instead of transportation.

8. **A start date**: The company will post when they expect you to start as an employee. This can be negotiated. Example: You and your spouse planned a trip that takes place the same week as the start date, negotiate to start upon your return from the trip, and explain why you need a different start date. If the company will not budge, ask if there is a specific reason. Maybe it is a deadline or project that is crucial to their company. You will have to consider all your options but if they are playing hardball and they do not give you a real reason for not allowing a couple of extra days to start, then you may have to reconsider whether you want to work for a company like that. You have options in the civilian world!

9. **Vacation days**: Most offer letters will state the number of vacation days a year. Always ask if vacation days get rolled over and added to the next year if not used. Also, ask if they buy back vacation days not used. And ask if they have a program where you can give or receive vacation days. Sometimes life throws you a curveball and you may need extra vacation days to recover.

   Now vacation time can be negotiated. Let say you wanted an extra $5,000 in salary but they said no. So, figure out your hourly wage and how many days you would need to work to make $5,000, Then ask for that amount of extra days added to your vacation total. And now you have technically given yourself a paid vacation.

10. **Response date**: Each offer letter or email will state that the company needs a response to their offer, and they will often put a time limit on this response. Usually, it is 2 days or 48 hours. You can negotiate for

more time but usually, they will give extra hours not days. There are many reasons why they do this, and it involves needing to fill the position and keeping other candidates open in case you reject their offer.

Remember once you sign the offer letter or send an acceptance email, you cannot negotiate any part of the offer. Always take your time, even if it is your dream job, and review, research and reassure yourself that this is what you need and want.

How to Accept a Job Offer

Graciously!!! Always accept a job offer in writing. Be grateful and appreciative of the opportunity and express this in your acceptance letter. This is a contract between the employer and you. Restate what is in the offer by writing in first-person format.

Example:

The offer letter was for an Operations Manager for Amazon. Then your first sentence would thank them for the offer and then you will reiterate that you will be their new Operations Manager and the location of this position.

Thank you for this opportunity and I look forward to being Amazon's Operation Manager at the Fort Worth Facility.

Then restate or verify that you will accept the items listed in your offer such as the amount for your salary, the number of vacation days, company allowances and even accepting the start date. So you will just restate what the offer says in your acceptance letter.

Template of an Acceptance Letter

{Your full name}

{Your address}

{City, State, and Zipcode}

{Date}

{Company's name}

{Address}

{City, State, and Zipcode}

Dear {Name of the person who sent the offer letter and their title}

Thank you for the opportunity to work as a {job title} for {Company name}. I am very pleased to accept this offer and I look forward to working with your company and everyone on my {team, division, branch}.

As the offer stated, my starting salary is {$ salary} and {Company name} will provide {List the benefits: Medical, vision, life insurance} after {days -usually 30 or up to 90 days of employment}. Also, I am appreciative of the {number} vacation {days or weeks} I will receive.

I look forward to my first day, {date} in my new career. If there is any additional paperwork or information you may need prior to my first day, please contact me at {phone number}

Respectfully,

{Full Name}

How to Negotiate a Job Offer

Do your research before approaching the company. Know the industry salary norm for your career and the job you applied for. Gather the information together to use in your letter. Also know the qualifications and experiences you are bringing to the company. If they only asked for five years of experience and you are bringing 20, then state this. If they asked for a bachelor's degree but you are bringing a master's degree, state this. Know your worth.

Template for a Negotiation Letter

{Your full name}

{Your address}

{City, State, and Zipcode)

{Date}

{Company's name}

{Address}

{City, State, and Zipcode}

Dear {Name of the person who sent the offer letter and their title}

I want to thank you for the offer to work at {company} as a {title}. I find the position to be an excellent opportunity to utilize my experiences and move forward with my career goals. Your company will provide me with an exciting environment to expand my qualifications in a significant way.

Before providing a formal acceptance, I would like to open a discussion concerning the salary base that you presented in my offer letter. The position of {title of job} is a very demanding and high-level position that I am fully capable of committing to. However, the base value that I bring to the company, plus my years of experience in a similar role for the Department of Defense {Branch}, along with the data attached to this email of similar titles in similar industries, I must ask that the company re-examine the salary offer presented to me. The annual range for this position based on the {data name} falls between {$$} and {$$} and I believe an offer of {$$} would be more consistent with my experience, qualifications, and the industry standard.

Respectfully,

{Full Name}

How to Reject a Job Offer

Always be grateful, humble, and appreciative in your rejection letter. You do not have to explain why you are rejecting this position or where you are going to work instead of this company.

Template for a Rejection Letter

{Your full name}

{Your address}

{City, State, and Zipcode)

{Date}

{Company's name}

{Address}

{City, State, and Zipcode}

Dear {Name of the person who sent the offer letter and their title}

I want to thank you for the offer to work at {company} as a {title}. I have decided to go a different route in my career path. Even though I will not be accepting this job offer, I wanted to let your company know I was honored to be chosen for this position.

I want to once again thank you for this opportunity.

Respectfully,

{Full Name}

WRAPPING UP MILITARY LIFE

The objectives of Chapter Thirteen

- To learn about resources that help with adjustment into civilian life

- To learn different ways to cope with situations in civilian life

- To understand the importance of networking to adjust to civilian life

- To learn of the different organizations available to help struggling veterans.

You are ready to become a civilian. The paperwork is done, the medical exam and approval to separate are complete, the resume has been accepted, the interview was successful, and you are ready to start your new civilian life. So, what now?

On paper, the transition sounds easy. It says that if you follow the checklist and do everything that is expected, your transition should be a great experience. But statistics tell a different story about the transition. Rich Morin's article "The Difficult Transition from Military to Civilian Life" shows that in a survey of 1,853 veterans, "While more than seven in ten veterans (72%) report they had an easy time readjusting to civilian life, 27% say re-entry was difficult for them—a proportion that swells to 44% among veterans who served in the ten years since the Sept. 11, 2001, terrorist attacks." (Morin, 2011)

Another article on "Readjusting to Civilian life" from 2019 states that "About half of veterans (47%) say they frequently felt optimistic about their future after leaving the military, 38% say they sometimes felt optimistic and 15% say they seldom or never felt this way. Here again, the findings differ by the era of service: 50% of pre-9/11 veterans say they frequently felt optimistic, compared with only a third of post-9/11 veterans. And roughly a quarter of post-9/11 veterans (23%) say they seldom or never felt optimistic about their future in the first few years after leaving the military." (Parker, Igielnik, Barroso and Cilluffo, 2019).

Challenges in Transitioning

Knowing that anywhere from 27% to 44% of veterans find readjustment to civilian life after the military difficult, means that there exist common struggles among veterans to adapt to the civilian world.

Let us examine some common struggles that have been found among transitioning veterans:

1. **Combat experience**

   "Veterans who served in combat are significantly more likely than those who did not to say their readjustment was difficult: 46% of those with some combat experience, compared with 18% of those without combat experience, describe their readjustment to civilian life as difficult" (Parker, Igielnik, Barroso and Cilluffo, 2019).

2. **Combat injury or disability**

   "One-in-five veterans say they, themselves, were seriously injured while performing their military duties: 5% say they were injured in combat and an additional 15% say their injury was not combat-related. Among veterans who have had combat experience, 16% say they were seriously injured in combat." (Parker, Igielnik, Barroso and Cilluffo, 2019.)

3. **Serving more than 20 years/rank differences**

   "Veterans who served as commissioned officers are more likely to say the military prepared them well for the transition to civilian life than are those who served as NCOs or as enlisted personnel (67% vs. 48% and 54%, respectively)." (Parker, Igielnik, Barroso and Cilluffo, 2019.)

4. **Serving after 9/11/2001**

   "Fully 68% of post-9/11 veterans with combat experience say their deployments helped them financially, compared with 30% of pre-9/11 combat veterans. But they are also more likely to say their deployments negatively impacted their mental health: About half of post-9/11 combat veterans (52%) say this, compared with 28% of pre-9/11 combat veterans." (Parker, Igielnik, Barroso and Cilluffo, Deployment 2019.)

5. **Veteran of both OIF and OEF**

   "Fully 44% of combat veterans say they believe they have suffered from PTS as a result of their military experience, compared with 8% of non-combat veterans. Among combat veterans, 55% of those who served after 9/11 say they have suffered from PTS, compared with 38% of those who served only before 9/11." (Parker, Igielnik, Barroso and Cilluffo, Deployment 2019.)

6. **Traumatic experience**

   "Roughly half of those who had traumatic experiences (53%) and an even higher share of those who say they have suffered from PTS (66%) say their readjustment was at least somewhat difficult. Among those with PTS, three-in-ten say it was very difficult." (Parker, Igielnik, Barroso and Cilluffo, 2019.)

7. **Grieving the loss of peers to combat deaths or suicide**

   "Roughly three-quarters of combat veterans (74%) say they know someone who was seriously injured while in the military, compared with 41% of veterans without combat experience. …Fully 57% of combat veterans say they personally witnessed someone from their unit or an ally unit being seriously wounded or killed." (Parker, Igielnik, Barroso and Cilluffo, Deployment 2019.)

8. **Survivor's guilt**

   "Relatedly, 31% of all veterans who know and served with someone who was killed while performing their duties say they have suffered from PTS, compared with 10% of those who don't know someone who was killed. That number jumps to 50% among post-9/11 veterans who know someone who was killed." (Parker, Igielnik, Barroso and Cilluffo, Deployment 2019.)

9. **Development of addiction issues**

   "One-in-five veterans say they struggled with alcohol or substance abuse in the first few years after leaving the military. Similar shares of post-9/11 (24%) and pre-9/11 (19%) veterans say they dealt with this issue." (Parker, Igielnik, Barroso and Cilluffo, 2019.)

10. **Lack of counseling or therapy for trauma**

    "About half of all combat veterans (52%) say they had emotionally traumatic experiences related to their military service. Post-9/11 combat veterans are especially likely to say this (62%). About three-in-ten combat veterans (31%) say they sought help for emotional issues resulting from their service, compared with 8% of veterans without combat experience." (Parker, Igielnik, Barroso and Cilluffo, 2019.)

11. **Warfare MOS such as infantry, sniper, artillery, etc.**

    "While most post-9/11 veterans say their military service was an advantage when it came to getting their post-military job, many say that job was not a perfect fit. About four-in-ten (42%) say they felt overqualified for their first job after leaving the military based on their skills, experience, and training; 46% say their qualifications were about right, and 12% felt underqualified." (Parker, Igielnik, Barroso and Cilluffo, 2019.)

12. **Going from war zone deployment to civilian transition with no deescalating time before separating**

    "Among veterans who were deployed, 23% say their deployments had a negative impact on their physical health, and an identical share say being deployed impacted their mental health negatively (Parker, Igielnik, Barroso and Cilluffo, 2019)"

13. **Lack of pride in their service or loss of pride in being a veteran**

"Roughly two-thirds of all veterans (68%) say, in the first few years after leaving the military, they frequently felt proud of their military service. An additional 22% say they sometimes felt proud, and 9% say they seldom or never felt this way. Pre-9/11 veterans are more likely to say they frequently felt proud of their service than are post-9/11 veterans (70% vs. 58%)." (Parker, Igielnik, Barroso and Cilluffo, 2019.)

14. **Lack of structure in civilian world creates stress**

"About one-in-ten veterans overall (9%) say they frequently had difficulty dealing with the lack of structure in civilian life after leaving the military, and an additional 23% say they sometimes felt this way. About two-thirds say they seldom (24%) or never (43%) had difficulty with this. Post-9/11 veterans are more likely than those who served in earlier eras to say they frequently had difficulty dealing with the lack of structure in civilian life (23% vs. 6%)." (Parker, Igielnik, Barroso and Cilluffo, 2019.)

15. **Belief that the Military did not adequately prepare veteran for civilian life**

"Some 16% say the military prepared them very well for the transition and 36% say it prepared them somewhat well. At the same time, more than four-in-ten say the military did not prepare them too well (30%) or at all (15%)." (Parker, Igielnik, Barroso and Cilluffo, 2019.)

16. **Race or gender**

"White veterans are much less likely than nonwhite veterans to report that, after leaving the military, they had trouble paying bills or accessing health care, or that they received unemployment or government food assistance. About half of nonwhite veterans (49%) say they had trouble paying bills in the first few years after leaving the military, compared with 32% of white veterans. And nonwhite veterans are more likely than white veterans to say they had trouble getting medical care for themselves or their family (29% vs. 12%). Male veterans are about twice as likely as female veterans to say they struggled with alcohol or substance abuse after leaving the military (21% vs. 10%). Female veterans are more likely to have received food assistance than their male counterparts – 24% of women vs. 11% of men say they received benefits such as WIC or SNAP from the government in the first few years after leaving the military." (Parker, Igielnik, Barroso and Cilluffo, 2019.)

I hope that by looking through at the studies done by Kim Parker, Ruth Igielnik, Amanda Barroso, and Anthony Cilluffo in 2019, you can see that many veterans are struggling with similar issues in the civilian world. In the next section, let us look at resources to assist and prepare for the challenges veterans may face after they separate from the military.

Obstacles Faced in Transition

In March of 2020, Laura Close wrote an article called "Veterans' struggles after Military Service" for the VeteranAddiction.org website. She states that the issues faced by veterans include physical and mental health, employment and financial struggles plus issues that can lead to homelessness. Her article breaks down the ways each of these factors can escalate for veterans during the transition. She found in her research that four factors have eased the transition to civilian life and those include being religious or spiritual, having leadership training in the service, being or seeking an education beyond high school, and having awareness for the reasons one was sent to combat, deployment or hostile environments for service.

The USC's Center for Innovation and Research on Veterans and Military Families (CIR) at the Suzanne Dworak-Peck School of Social Work conducted a series of studies in 2017 on the process of transition with various military members and their families in California. The studies uncovered similar findings that showed the lack of preparedness for transition and the lack of understanding of what to expect of the civilian world, which led to the greatest challenges for veterans (USC Suzanne Dworak-Peck School of Social Work, 2017).

In 2020, due to the COVID-19 quarantine, the Transition Assistance Program (TAP) was solely given online. The online version was not beneficial for many transitioning militaries. The online version cannot receive one-on-one help from presenters who are trained to discuss resumes, job searches, and interviews. Activities completed in the in-person training allowed the service member to practice their skills for interviewing, a 30-second job fair pitch, and even resume writing with peers and skilled trainers. The ability to discuss skills and how to read the VMET information is important and often missed in the online pieces of training. Also, the lack of understanding of the resources available or missing the key information of what is available can occur in online training.

In February of 2020, Jennifer Barnhill wrote an article for Military.com on "Problems with the Military Transition Process Need More than a Band-Aid Solution," where she discussed that there exists "High-profile reports on veteran suicide, homelessness, incarceration, and depression have tightened the coil, leaving many veterans service organizations, politicians and federal agencies ready to spring into (re)action (Barnhill, 2020)."

Barnhill discussed a new style of transition programs that were introduced by Marine veteran Ron Shelf, founder of Veterans Healing Veterans from the Inside Out (VHV) at https://veteranshealingveterans.com/index.html. He designed a program which he calls: Boots Camp Out, that would work with veteran in peer-to-peer capacity with different therapies, coping strategies, and of course financial planning and resume writing workshops (Barnhill, 2020). "According to Self, without a program like Boot Camp Out, the military is essentially bringing a tank back from a combat zone, painting it yellow and calling it a school bus. It is a weapon of war; so is the veteran. Not addressing this head-on during the military-civilian transition puts service members and everyone they encounter at-risk (Barnhill, 2020)."

Another issue Barnhill discovered is that many military service members withhold injury, medical and PTSD symptoms for fear of being disqualified for promotion or discharged. Some service members go years without treatment for symptoms that are treatable but are perceived as a weakness or carries a stigma in the military (Barnhill, 2020). Transition programs should build confidence in the service member to find treatment before exiting the military and to not feel penalized for doing so.

Four key areas are found to be the most difficult to navigate for military transitioning members:

1. **Connecting to services in the civilian world**

   Understanding where to find the services, who to trust, and what is expected for payment. The services can range from finding a new barber to doctors and dentists. Establishing a relationship with providers of services can be challenging but if service members find this part difficult or that it creates anxiety for them, then they are encouraged to seek out an anxiety specialist. A trained professional in this area is key to help them gain coping skills to navigate this challenge.

2. **Establishing structure or a routine**

   Routines that were structured in the military will not exist in the civilian world. There are no consequences or reprimands if you are not dressed correctly. It is on the veteran to create their schedule. Create a schedule with times and responsibilities that require your presence. Add PT into your schedule and chow time. Make sure you get up and get dressed. Using a list to checkoff responsibilities is a great way to establish a daily routine.

3. **Relationship and network building**

   Civilians will not understand a veteran. They have not lived in that environment. They cannot possibly understand what your experience has been. Forgive them for this ignorance. Do not isolate yourself from your new world. Meet and form new connections. Join teams, go to meet-ups, find a hobby, go to a gym, and reconnect with veterans in the civilian world through organizations. If you find that you are struggling to be received or included in the civilian world, talk with a seasoned veteran who has navigated the civilian world. Ask them for mentorship on how to meet and network. Just do not isolate and exclude yourself from your place in the world. The world needs you and your skills/experiences. Finding the right fit means changing tactics and strategies to discover the best route for you.

4. **Finding Civilian Employment**

   This whole guidebook has discussed all the issues and methods a military service member can experience when seeking a civilian career. As we discussed in previous chapters, the civilian world has no clue what experiences you have or what it means to serve in warzones. They have no idea the detailed workloads or responsibilities you carried in your MOS. Your resume needs to showcase your skills and experiences in a way that makes it clear to the civilian recruiter or HR manager what you can do for them. You need to keep your humor when applying for civilian work because what is considered difficult for the civilian is a relaxing day for the military member. Remember you are very prepared for civilian work, you just need to show them on paper and then in the interview the great skills and experiences you bring to their company.

Veteran Homelessness

Laura Close found through a 2018 study from "Homelessness in America" that 9% of homeless people in America are veterans. And out of those 9%, 38% of those veterans live on the street or in their car. (Close, 2020.)

Let us look at the causes, or situations that led to homelessness

1. **Traumatic experience**

2. **Unemployment or being unable to hold a job**

3. **Economic hardship**

4. **Relationship problems**

5. **Family isolation or estrangement**

6. **Lack of counseling or therapy for trauma**

7. **Addiction issues**

Close's article discussed the stigma surrounding being homeless in America. Homelessness is a situational problem, not a choice. The VA has programs in place to help find housing for any veteran of the American armed forces. Below are a few groups that can help veterans with finding housing or shelter:

The VA Community Resource and Referral Centers (CTTCs) at www.va.gov/HOMELESS/Crrc.asp

The United Way offers help at www.211.org

National Coalition for Homeless Veterans has a veteran page of resources at https://nchv.org/index.php/help

HUD Exchange www.hudexchange.info/homelessness-assistance/resources-for-homeless-veterans/

Housing help for Veterans at www.usa.gov/veteran-housing

US VA Benefits page discusses sources to help homeless veterans at www.benefits.va.gov/persona/veteran-homeless.asp

NVTAC discusses the Homeless Veterans Reintegration Program (HVRP) on its site at https://nvtac.org/grantees/welcome-new-grantees/

We Got Your Six at https://wgy6.org is a non-profit organization dedicated to helping homeless Veterans

Transition Stress

Many veterans experience periods of stress during their transition from the military. Some of the stressors include:

1. **Emotions attached to their separation**

   Many veterans grieve the end of their service, the loss of friends and networks, and their status or responsibilities. Feelings of being overwhelmed with their new civilian roles, family expectations, and social placement can create stress.

2. **Memories of Service**

   With more time to think and analyze, memories of service, combat missions, and operations may resurface and often can be idealized or traumatizing. Analyzing these memories can cause stress. Seeking treatment for traumatic memories is encouraged.

3. **Emotions attached to actions in service**

   Feelings of shame, guilt, sadness, and anger over experiences or actions while serving in the military may surface after separating.

4. **Negative perceptions of veterans**

   Veterans who remove themselves from military places find the perception of the military is very different in the civilian world. Especially in places not familiar with the military or near military installations. Some emotions can surface such as pride issues, fear, anger, and even sadness over how civilians see veterans and the military.

5. **Stereotyping a soldier or veteran**

   Gender stereotypes or masculine gender stereotyping veterans and expecting a certain character to exist because of service. Feelings of not fitting in, letting others down, or living a non-authentic life can surface.

PTSD/TBI and Depression

The fact is that there are mental health concerns for veterans after separating. Depression affects more service members and veterans than civilians. Anxiety and excessive worry can dominate a veteran's life and cause a multitude of problems including insomnia, professional and personal issues, relationship challenges, and can lead to other health problems.

Traumatic Brain Injury or TBI is a head injury that occurs from being near or around artillery, bombs, IUDs, or other blasts that affected the brain's regular function. Post-traumatic Stress Disorder or PTSD is a mental illness that develops in response to a traumatic event, assault, or witnessing a volatile situation. The body responds by using its "fight-or-flight" function.

PTSD and TBI can develop over time and many veterans find that they can exhibit the symptoms related to this disorder sometimes years after separating from the military.

PTSD symptoms:

- Repeated memories of events
- Isolation and avoidance of people or interactions

- Avoidance of sounds or places that resemble the memory

- Survivor's guilt

- Flashbacks that are often caused by sudden triggers such as smells, sounds, or places

- Relieving the event through flashbacks

- Haunting thoughts and memories that constantly occur

- Constant alertness or hypervigilance

- Worry, anxiety, and panic over events, people, or places

- Fear of being unsafe or life-threatening events

- Emotional numbness/shutdown/unresponsive

- Shame and extreme sadness over events

- Impairments/neurological disorders affecting vision, hearing, behaviors, communication, cognitive learning, memory, social skills, and smell.

TBI symptoms:

- A period of amnesia after the event that caused the injury where the person cannot remember the event, the time before or right after

- Sleep disorders, insomnia, and disruption of sleep patterns

- Social isolation

- Extreme fatigue

- Changes in cognitive abilities, difficulty in learning or speaking

- Unpredictable emotions

- Depression/mood disorders

- Anxiety and anger/can be volatile if damage occurred to the frontal lobes of the brain

- Slow or delayed reaction, speech, and cognitive thinking

- Loss of sensation

As mentioned in Chapter 3, the VA offers: https://www.publichealth.va.gov/exposures/health-concerns.asp

- PTSD treatment – https://www.ptsd.va.gov/

- Traumatic Brain Injury – https://www.ptsd.va.gov/professional/treat/cooccurring/tbi_ptsd_vets.asp

- Blindness Rehabilitation – https://www.rehab.va.gov/PROSTHETICS/blindrehab/locations.asp

- Agent Orange Exposure – https://www.va.gov/disability/eligibility/hazardous-materials-exposure/agent-orange/

- Gulf War Syndrome and illnesses SW Asia – https://www.va.gov/disability/eligibility/hazardous-materials-exposure/gulf-war-illness-southwest-asia/

- Gulf War Illnesses Afghanistan – https://www.va.gov/disability/eligibility/hazardous-materials-exposure/gulf-war-illness-afghanistan/

- Substance Abuse and Mental Health Services – https://www.samhsa.gov/

Veteran Suicide Risk

The number one reason why veterans think about or attempt suicide is to end "intense emotional distress." (Military Suicide Research Consortium, 2020.) The Pentagon-funded study "shows that suicide rates in the military were highest among people divorced or separated — with a rate of 19 per 100,000 — 24% higher than troops who are single. Besides, mental health rates have risen 65% in the military since 2000, with 936,000 troops diagnosed with at least one mental health issue in that time, according to the new data." (Military Suicide Research Consortium. 2020.)

Warning Signs/Suicidal Tendencies

- Feeling hopeless

- Insomnia/exhaustion

- Lack of eating

- Anxious, annoyed, or agitated all the time

- Rage or constant anger

- Addiction or substance abuse

- Withdrawal or seclusion from others

(Please note, counseling or reaching out to get professional help should be a priority if you witness or experience any of these signs.)

Seek help immediately if you…

- Are imagining harming yourself

- Are planning on attempting to self-harm

- Are taking risks without thinking or caring about consequences

- Are behaving violently towards self or others

- Feel uncontrolled rage or anger

- Have a death wish which is evident through actions or voicing this wish

- Are giving away treasured items, belongings, or money

- Seek weapons, pills, or other means to harm oneself

- Are researching how to harm self

- Have voiced or have told someone that you want to hurt yourself

Where to find support

The VA has programs to help connect veterans with counselors and suicide prevention specialists at www.mental-health.va.gov/MENTALHEALTH/suicide_prevention/index.asp or through a confidential support line that is 24/7 at the Veterans Crisis Line at **1-800-273-8255 and Press 1.**

Also, many veterans have started non-profits to help prevent veteran suicide. Here are a few organizations that have helped thousands of veterans find support and relief from these thoughts and feelings:

Make the Connection at www.maketheconnection.net/conditions/suicide

DOD Safe Helpline for Transitioning Military or Active Military Sexual Trauma Survivors can talk to someone for help at 1-877-995-5247 or online https://safehelpline.org

RestoreLifeGlobal.com is a suicide prevention organization started by a Navy Veteran, Porsche Williams, who has made it her mission to train people on how to recognize the warning signs of suicide. She teaches a two-day interactive workshop called Applied Suicide Intervention Skills Training (ASIST) at www.restorelifeglobal.com.

American Foundation for Suicide Prevention has a Crisis line at **1-800-273-8255 or text to TALK at 741741.**

#BeHereTomorrow at https://suicidology.org/facts-and-statistics/

Suicide Hotline: **1-800-784-2433 (1-800-SUICIDE**

Things to actively do to prevent suicidal tendencies

1. Surround yourself with loved ones, family, friends, battle buddies, other veterans, co-workers. Talk, communicate and reach out for interaction with others.

2. Set goals to accomplish every day that are realistic and practical—exercise goals, hobby goals, travel goals, work goals, project goals, and even financial goals.

3. Volunteer to help those less fortunate or in need. Sometimes having a purpose greater than ourselves can help us find a reason to be in the moment and here.

4. Learning coping mechanism: meditation, prayer, karate, yoga, journaling, arts, music, reiki, EFT, counseling, singing, dancing, exercising, writing, and even public speaking

5. Find spirituality, a source greater than oneself. Look at joining or rejoining a religious organization, become active, join prayer groups, social events and be part of their community.

6. Relax, take a vacation, be in nature, get pampered, and breathe.

7. Find a meeting or a group to join such as Veteran support, Wounded Warriors, even AA, NA, or other health or social type of groups.

8. Counseling, talk therapy, pastoral counseling, or therapy.

9. Look for alternative approaches to dealing with emotional distress such as changing your diet, CBD oil, working with a naturopathic doctor, shaman, life coach, massage therapy, EMDR, process healing method, SRT, vibration or emotional psychology treatment, and contemporary healing modalities.

10. Be of service to others:

    a. Work with at-risk kids, tutor, coach, or mentoring a child who has been through a rough experience can be inspiring. To volunteer as a sports coach, see Semper Fi Sports at www.semper-fi-sports.org

       At-risk children can also deal with similar PTSD and trauma that combat soldiers know, and this is too due to living near or being a part of gang violence or domestic violence. The American Psychological Association conducted a 2016 study that found "Nearly all youth detained in the juvenile justice system have experienced traumatic events often leading to Post-Traumatic Stress Disorder (PTSD) and comorbid disorders." (Bushman et al. 2016.) A common link between veterans and at-risk youth has been noted and programs to connect these two populations has been found to help both overcome adversity and prevents suicide. Read more about this topic at the National Center for the Prevention of Youth Suicide at www.preventyouthsuicide.org.

    b. Work with or be mentored by elderly veterans, especially Korean and Vietnam veterans who have experienced similar combat military operations. The VA has volunteer programs to drive veterans to appointments, delivering food to them through programs, to help with daily chores such as mowing their lawns, going shopping for them, or taking them to shop. Many elderly people are shut-ins, especially during COVID-19 and volunteering to check on their safety is crucial. The elderly suicide rate has grown more than 30% and many do not have the necessities to seek help such as transportation, medical insurance, or even a phone to call (Aginginplace.org, 2021).

    c. Volunteer with a non-profit:

       • Habitat for Humanity at www.habitat.org/volunteer

       • American Legion at www.legion.org/volunteers

       • Disabled American Veterans at https://auxiliary.dav.org/volunteer/

       • Volunteer Transportation Network at www.volunteer.va.gov/VolTransNetwork.asp

       • Operation Gratitude at www.operationgratitude.com

       • Angel Wings for Veterans at https://angelwingsforveterans.org

- Soldiers' Angels at soldiersangels.org/volunteer/

- Saving our Vets at https://savingourvets.org/volunteer/

- Harbor Hospice at harborhospicemi.org/ways-to-give/volunteer/

- VeteransInc, at www.veteransinc.org/donations/volunteers/

- Veterans Moving Forward at https://vetsfwd.org/volunteer/

- USO at www.uso.org/take-action/volunteer

- VFW at www.vfw.org/community/community-initiatives/volunteer-service

- Wounded Warrior Project at www.woundedwarriorproject.org

- National Cemetery Administration at www.cem.va.gov/VolunteerNCA.asp or other various groups that need help.

Military Discrimination

Qualified veterans and active reservists have been turned away from positions due to their military affiliation. A negative attitude from the civilian sector towards those who have worn the uniform of our military has been reported. Lack of education for HR managers, generalists, and recruiters about the business side of the Department of Defense has led to stereotyping by HR people towards veterans. In 2021, many transitioning veterans have reported this discrimination is still occurring. In 2012, the Obama administration created the Returning Heroes and Wounded Warrior Tax Credit that offered employers a tax incentive to hire veterans. The company would receive up to $5600 for hiring an unemployed veteran and the Wounded Warrior tax credit is $9600 for hiring a service-connected disabled veteran (Military.com, 2012).

LinkedIn provided a Veteran Opportunity Report for 2021 which explored the effectiveness of veteran-hiring practices. They found out that veterans usually remained with the company longer and were more likely to be promoted to leadership roles. And veterans were more likely to achieve graduate degrees and have more work experience than nonveterans (LinkedIn, 2021).

If you run into a situation where you feel you have been discriminated against due to your military affiliation you do have legal rights and a lawyer should be consulted.

"The **Uniformed Services Employment and Reemployment Rights Act (USERRA)** of 2011 prohibits **employment discrimination** based on an employee's past, present, or future military service. This federal law applies to anyone who performs duties in the "uniformed services," whether involuntarily or voluntarily. The "uniformed services" include the Army, Marine Corps, Navy, Army National Guard, Coast Guard, Air Force, Air National Guard, or Public Health Service commissioned corps. Certain disaster work also counts as uniformed service and qualifies an employee for protection under USERRA." (Justia.com, 2021.)

Conclusion

You have gone through the entire guidebook with its wealth of information to assist you in your transition. You have all the tools, resources, and connections to confidently move into a civilian career. I am so honored you have purchased my guidebook to help you with this endeavor.

This decision is about what is best for you and your loved one and I hope by using this guidebook, you are getting informed and prepared for your life-altering career move.

Thank you and best wishes,
Angela

ABOUT THE AUTHOR

Angela Gunshore is a coach, educator, published author, and facilitator with experience working in the academic, corporate, military, and non-profit sectors. She holds Master's degrees in Psychology and History/Social Science as well as certifications in education, coaching, and holistic therapies. Her goal is to mentor and coach clients in all sectors of life transitions including career exploration, professional development, relationship changes, holistic focus, and personal goal setting.

Visit her website at www.angelgunshore.com to learn more about her career coaching approach

BIBLIOGRAPHY

123Test.Com. (2021). *Career Test - Free Online Aptitude Test - 123test.Com.* 123test.Com. Https://Www.123test. Com/Career-Test/

16 Personalities. (2021). *"It's So Incredible To Finally Be Understood." Free Personality Test, Type Descriptions, Relationship, And Career Advice |.* 16Personalities.

Https://Www.16personalities.Com

ACE. (2021). *American Council on Education Homepage.* American Council on Education. Https://Www.Acenet.Edu

Air Force Virtual Education Center, B. (2021). *Air Force COOL.* AFVEC. Https://Afvec.Us.Af.Mil/Afvec/Af-Cool/ Welcome

Air Force. (2019, April 19). *Community College of The Air Force Transcripts.* Air University (AU). Https://Www.Airuniversity.Af.Edu/Barnes/CCAF/Display/Article/803247/ Community-College-Of-The-Air-Force-Transcripts/

Amazon. (2021). *Military Pathways 2021 - Nationwide Opportunities (United States).* Amazon.Jobs. Https:// Amazon.Jobs/En/Jobs/1194531/Military-Pathways-2021-Nationwide-Opportunities-United-States

American Express. (2021). *Service Members Civil Relief |.* American Express Credit Cards, Rewards & Banking. Https://Www.Americanexpress.Com/Us/Help-Support/Service-Members-Civil-Relief/

AMU. (2021). *Freedom Grant.* American Military University. Https://Start.Amu.Apus.Edu/Freedom-Grant/ Overview?Utm_Source=Military-Base&Utm_Medium=Banner&Utm_Content=Freedom-Grant&Utm_ Campaign=AMU%20-%20DT%20-%20AMU

Assessment.Com. (2021). *Home of The MAPP Assessment -* Https://Www.Assessment.Com/?Accnum=06-5329-000.00

Bank of America. (2021). *Military Benefits FAQs: Deployment, Management, & SCRA.* Https://Www.Bankofamerica. Com/Military-Banking/Military-Banking-Faqs/

Barnhill, J. (2020, February 6). *Problems with the military transition process need more than a band-aid solution.* Military.com. https://www.military.com/daily-news/2020/02/06/problems-military-transition-process-need-more-band-aid-solution.html

Beshara, T. (2014). *Powerful Phrases for Successful Interviews: Over 400 Ready-To-Use Words And Phrases That Will Get You The Job You Want.* AMACOM Books

BOEING. (2021). *Apprenticeship*. IAM/Boeing Joint Apprenticeship. Https://Www.Iam-Boeing-Apprenticeship. Com/

Bushman, B. J., Newman, K., Calvert, S. L., Downey, G., Dredze, M., Gottfredson, M., Jablonski, N. G., Masten, A. S., Morrill, C., Neill, D. B., Romer, D., & Webster, D. W. (2016). Youth violence: What we know and what we need to know. *American Psychologist*, *71*(1), 17-39. https://doi.org/10.1037/a0039687

Capital One. (2021). *Servicemembers Civil Relief Act*. Capital One Credit Cards, Bank, and Loans - Personal and Business. Https://Www.Capitalone.Com/Military/Faqs

Career Explorer. (2021). *Unlock the Future You*. Career explorer. Https://Www.Careerexplorer.Com/Assessments/

Careermaze. (2021). *Assessment 10 Minute*. Https://Www.Careermaze.Com

Careeronestop. (2021). *Civilian-To-Military-Translator*. Https://Www.Careeronestop.Org/Businesscenter/Toolkit/ Civilian-To-Military-Translator.Aspx

Careeronestop. (2021). *Skill-Matcher*. Https://www.Careeronestop.Org/Toolkit/Skills/Skills-Matcher.Aspx

Careerscope. (2021). *GI Bill*. Career scope Assessment Portal. Https://Va.Careerscope.Net/Gibill

Chase.Com. (2021). *SCRA | Military |*. Credit Card, Mortgage, Banking, Auto | Chase Online | Chase.Com. Https:// Www.Chase.Com/Digital/Military/Scra

Close, L. (2020, March 23). *The challenging transition from military to civilian life | VeteranAddiction.org*. veteranaddiction.org. https://veteranaddiction.org/veterans-struggles-after-military-service

Cummins HR Department. (2021). *Explore Our Opportunities at Cummins*. Cummins Apprenticeship Jobs. Https:// Cummins-Apprenticeship.Jobs/

DANTES. (2021). *Defense Voluntary Education Programs*. Defense Activity for Non-Traditional Education Support (DANTES). Https://Www.Dantes.Doded.Mil/

Department of Veteran Affairs. (2019). *Understanding PTSD Treatment*. PTSD: National Center for PTSD Home. https://www.ptsd.va.gov/understand_tx/index.asp

Department of Veteran Affairs. (2021). *VA Form 21P-530 Application for Burial Benefits*. Veterans Benefits Administration Home. Https://Www.Vba.Va.Gov/Pubs/Forms/VBA-21P-530-ARE.Pdf

Department of Veteran Affairs. (2021). *VA Form 40-1330M Government Medallion for Placement in a Private Cemetery*. Veterans Benefits Administration Home. Https://Www.Va.Gov/Vaforms/Va/Pdf/VA40-1330M.Pdf

Department of Veteran Affairs. (2021). *VA Form 40-40007 Pre-Need Determination of Eligibility for Burial in a VA National Cemetery*. VA.Gov Veterans Affairs. Https://Www.Va.Gov/Vaforms/Va/Pdf/VA40-10007.Pdf

Department of Veterans Affairs. (N.D.). *VA Form 28-8832 Educational/Vocational Counseling Application*. Veterans Benefits Administration Home. Https://Www.Vba.Va.Gov/Pubs/Forms/VBA-28-8832-ARE.Pdf

Discover. (2021). *SCRA Benefits Login | Credit Card Benefits for U.S. Servicemembers | Discover*. Discover - Card Services, Banking & Loans. Https://Www.Discover.Com/Credit-Cards/Member-Benefits/Scra-Benefits/

DOD. (2014, January 24). *Job Training, Employment Skills Training, Apprenticeships, And Internships (JTEST-AI) For Eligible Service Members.* DOD SkillBridge. Https://Dodskillbridge.Usalearning.Gov/Docs/Announcement-Career-Skills-Program-JTESTAI-Program.Pdf

DOD. (2020, November 25). *DOD SkillBridge Homepage.* DOD SkillBridge. Https://Dodskillbridge.Usalearning.Gov

DOD. (2020, October 8). *SkillBridge Program Participant Ethics Brief.* DOD SkillBridge. Https://Dodskillbridge.Usalearning.Gov/Docs/Skillbridge-Program-Participant-Ethics-Brief-V2.Pptx

DOD. (2021). *Servicemembers Civil Relief Act (SRCA.* SCRA. Https://Scra.Dmdc.Osd.Mil/Scra/#/Home

DOD. (2021). *Joint Service Transcripts (JST).* Department of Defense. Https://Jst.Doded.Mil/Jst/

DOD. (2021). *Veteran Support Organizations.* U.S. Department of Defense. Https://Www.Defense.Gov/Resources/Veteran-Support-Organizations/

DOJ. (2020, October 23). *The Servicemembers Civil Relief Act (SCRA).* Department of Justice. Https://Www.Justice.Gov/Servicemembers/Servicemembers-Civil-Relief-Act-Scra

DOL. (2017). *U.S. DOL Employment Workshop.* Transition Assistance Program/U.S. Department of Labor.

DOL. (2018). *Career Exploration and Planning Track Participant Guide.* Transition Assistance Program/US Department of Labor

DOL. (2019, November 1). *Unemployment Compensation for Ex-Servicemembers.* Unemployment Insurance Benefit Payments, Employment & Training Administration (ETA) - U.S. Department of Labor. Https://Oui.Doleta.Gov/Unemploy/Ucx.Asp

DOL. (2021). *Licensing and Certification for Veterans: State Strategies for Successfully Removing Barriers.* U.S. Department of Labor. Https://Www.Dol.Gov/Sites/Dolgov/Files/VETS/Legacy/Files/Licensingcertfications.Pdf

DOL. (2021). *Service Members and Veterans.* Apprenticeship.Gov. Https://www.Apprenticeship.Gov/Career-Seekers/Service-Members-And-Veterans

DOL. (2021). *Veterans.Gov | Veterans' Employment and Training Service (VETS) -.* U.S. Department of Labor. Https://www.Veterans.Gov

DOL. (2021). *Apprenticeship.* U.S. Department of Labor. Https://www.Dol.Gov/Agencies/Eta/Apprenticeship

Editors of Aginginplace.org. (2019, September 12). *Elderly suicide: The risks, detection, and how to help.* AgingInPlace.org. https://aginginplace.org/elderly-suicide-risks-detection-how-to-help/

Enelow, W. S., & Kursmark, L. (2011). *Expert Resumes for Managers and Executives.* Jist Works.

Executive Services Directorate. (N.D.). *DD Form 2807 Report of Medical History.* Https://Www.Esd.Whs.Mil/Portals/54/Documents/DD/Forms/Dd/Dd2807-1.Pdf

FAA. (2019, May 17). *For Veterans.* Federal Aviation Administration. Https://Www.Faa.Gov/Jobs/Working_Here/Veterans/

FAA. (2020, April 6). *Air Carrier and Air Agency Certification*. Federal Aviation Administration. Https://Www. Faa.Gov/Licenses_Certificates/Airline_Certification/

Falcone, P. (2005). *2600 Phrases for Effective Performance Reviews: Ready-To-Use Words and Phrases That Really Get Results*. AMACOM/American Management Association.

Farr, J. M. (2007). *Top 100 Careers for College Graduates: Your Complete Guidebook to Major Jobs in Many Fields*. JIST Works.

Fedvte. (2021). *Fedvte Course Catalog*. Federal Virtual Training Environment. Https://Fedvte.Usalearning.Gov/ Coursecat_External.Php

Fry, R. W. (2000). *101 Great Answers to The Toughest Interview Questions*. Delmar Pub

GE Careers. (2021, March 3). *Students at GE | GE Careers*. Jobs at GE | GE Building a World That Works. Https:// Jobs.Gecareers.Com/Global/En/Students

GE Healthcare. (2021). *Apprentice Jobs*. GE Healthcare Systems | GE Healthcare. Https://Www.Gehealthcare. Com/About/Apprentice-Job

General Electric. (2021, March 25). *Explore Your Future*. Jobs at GE | GE Building A World That Works. Https://Jobs.Gecareers.Com/Power/Global/En/Job/GE11GLOBALR3539934EXTERNALENGLOBAL/ Machinist-Apprentice-Program

Google. (2021). *IT Support Certificate Training Program - Grow with Google*. Grow with Google. Https://Grow. Google/Programs/It-Support/#?Modal_Active=None

Hay, M. T., Rorrer, L. H., & Rivera, J. R. (2005). *Military Transition to Civilian Success: The Complete Guide for Veterans and Their Families*.

Heimbuch, K. (2021). IMAGE *Navy officer hugs wife*. Pixabay.

Hire Heroes. (2020, September 28). *Training Partners*. Hire Heroes USA. Https://Www.Hireheroesusa.Org/ Training-Partners/

HRCI. (2021). *HRCI Certification for Military HR Personnel*. Https://Www.Hrci.Org/Our-Programs/ Certify-Your-Staff/Certification-For-Military-Hr-Personnel

Humanmetrics -. (2021). *Personality Test Based on C. Jung And I. Briggs Myers Type Theory*. Humanmetrics. Https://Www.Humanmetrics.Com/Cgi-Win/Jtypes2.Asp#Questionnaire

IACP. (2010). *Combat Veterans & Law Enforcement*. International Association of Chiefs of Police. Https://Www. Theiacp.Org/Sites/Default/Files/2018-08/Vetsguide_300dpi.Pdf

IJCSA. (2021). *Green Cleaning Certification*. International Janitorial Cleaning Services Association. Https://Www. Ijcsa.Org/Green-Cleaning-Certification/

IJCSA. (2021). *Hazardous Chemical Certification*. International Janitorial Cleaning Services Association. Https:// Www.Ijcsa.Org/Hazardous-Chemical-Certification/

IJCSA. (2021). *Master Janitorial Certification*. International Janitorial Cleaning Services Association. Https:// Www.Ijcsa.Org/Janitorial-Certification-Program/

IRS. (2020, 18). *Types of Retirement Plans*. Internal Revenue Service | An Official Website of The United States Government. Https://Www.Irs.Gov/Retirement-Plans/Plan-Sponsor/Types-Of-Retirement-Plans

IRS. (2021, February 12). *Publication 3 (2020), Armed Forces' Tax Guide*. Internal Revenue Service | An Official Website of The United States Government. Https://Www.Irs.Gov/Publications/P3#En_US_2015_Publink1000176279

IVMF Staff. (2021, March 8). *Learning Pathways*. Institute for Veterans and Military Families. Https://Ivmf. Syracuse.Edu/Programs/Career-Training/Learning-Pathways/

Justia.com. (2021, March 16). *Military status discrimination*. Justia. https://www.justia.com/employment/ employment-discrimination/military-status-discrimination/

Keirsey. (2021). *Keirsey Temperament Sorter*. Https://Profile.Keirsey.Com/#/B2c/Assessment/Start

LinkedIn. (2021). *Veteran opportunity report*. Social Impact | LinkedIn. https://socialimpact.linkedin.com/programs/ veterans/veteran-opportunity-report

LinkedIn. (2021). *Military & Veterans*. Social Impact | LinkedIn. Https://Socialimpact.Linkedin.Com/Programs/ Veterans

Lockheed Martin. (2021). *Apprenticeships with Lockheed Martin*. Search Jobs and Careers at Lockheed Martin Corporation. Https://Www.Lockheedmartinjobs.Com/Apprenticeships

Louis, M. J. (2019). *Mission Transition: Navigating the Opportunities and Obstacles to Your Post-Military Career*. Harper Collins Leadership.

Mantech. (2021). *For Transitioning Military*. Mantech Securing the Future. Https://Www.Mantech.Com/Careers/ Transitioning-Military

MI Staff. (N.D.). *Heroes MAKE America Training Program*. The Manufacturing Institute. Https://Www. Themanufacturinginstitute.Org/Veterans/Heroes-Make-America/Training-Program/

MIL Connect. (2021). *TRICARE*. Milconnect: Benefits and Records For DOD Affiliates. Https://Milconnect.Dmdc. Osd.Mil/Milconnect/

Military Health System. (2021). *Separation Health Assessment*. Https://Www.Health.Mil/Military-Health-Topics/Access-Cost-Quality-And-Safety/Access-To-Healthcare/Dod-VA-Sharing-Initiatives/ Separation-Health-Assessment

Military.com. (2012, March 8). *How to get tax credits for hiring veterans*. https://www.military.com/hiring-veterans/resources/tax-credits-for-hiring-veterans.html Military.Com. (2021). *Military Skills Translator*. Https:// Www.Military.Com/Veteran-Jobs/Skills-Translator

Military Suicide Research Consortium. (2020). *Study reveals top reason behind soldiers' suicides | Military suicide research consortium*. msrc.fsu.edu. https://msrc.fsu.edu/news/study-reveals-top-reason-behind-soldiers-suicides

Mobbs, M. C., & Bonanno, G. A. (2018). Beyond war and PTSD: The crucial role of transition stress in the lives of military veterans. *Clinical Psychology Review, 59*, 137-144. https://doi.org/10.1016/j.cpr.2017.11.007

Morin, R. (2011, December 8). *The difficult transition from military to civilian life.* Pew Research Center's Social & Demographic Trends Project. https://www.pewresearch.org/social-trends/2011/12/08/the-difficult-transition-from-military-to-civilian-life/

Murphey, R. (2017, March 2). *The difference between a TBI and PTSD.* MilitarySpot.com. https://www.militaryspot.com/community/difference-tbi-ptsd

My Next Move for Veterans. (2021). *What Do You Want to Do for a Living?* Https://Www.Mynextmove.Org/Vets/

National Center For PTSD. (2021). *PTSD: National Center For PTSD.* VA.Gov | Veterans Affairs. Https://Www.Ptsd.Va.Gov/

NAMI Staff. (2021). *Veterans & active duty | NAMI: National Alliance on Mental Illness.* NAMI: National Alliance on Mental Illness. https://www.nami.org/Your-Journey/Veterans-Active-Duty

NCMRS. (N.D.). *Financial Assistance, Interest-Free Loans & Scholarships.* Navy-Marine Corps Relief Society (NMCRS) -. Https://Www.Nmcrs.Org/

Northrop Grumman HR. (2020, July 31). *Jobs.* Northrop Grumman. Https://Www.Northropgrumman.Com/Jobs/

O*Net Online. (2021). *Military Crosswalk Search.* O*NET Online. Https://Www.Onetonline.Org/Crosswalk/MOC

O*Net Online. (2021). *Find Occupations.* Https://Www.Onetonline.Org/Find/

Office of Assistant Secretary for Information and Technology. (2021). *Home - VA/Dod Ebenefits.* Department of Veteran Affairs. Https://Www.Ebenefits.Va.Gov/Ebenefits-Portal

Onward to Opportunity. (2021, March 8). *Learning Pathways/O2O Courses.* Institute for Veterans and Military Families. Https://Ivmf.Syracuse.Edu/Programs/Career-Training/Learning-Pathways/

Onward to Opportunity. (2021, March 8). *Learning Pathways.* Institute for Veterans and Military Families. Https://Ivmf.Syracuse.Edu/Programs/Career-Training/Learning-Pathways/?Q=/Employment/Vctp-Certification-Paths/&

Parker, K., Igielnik, R., Barroso, A., & Cilluffo, A. (2019, December 31). *How veterans readjust to civilian life.* Pew Research Center's Social & Demographic Trends Project. https://www.pewresearch.org/social-trends/2019/09/09/readjusting-to-civilian-life/

Parker, K., Igielnik, R., Barroso, A., & Cilluffo, A. (2019, December 31). *How veterans feel about deployment and combat.* Pew Research Center's Social & Demographic Trends Project. https://www.pewresearch.org/social-trends/2019/09/09/deployment-combat-and-their-consequences/

Parker, Y. (2002). *The Damn Good Resume Guide: A Crash Course in Resume Writing.*

The Patriots Initiative. (2019, September 4). *Warriors in Transition: List of Companies for JMO And Pathways.* Https://Www.Thepatriotsinitiative.Org/Transition/Warriorsintransition/

PMI Staff. (2021). *Project Management Basics - An Official PMI Online Course.* Program Management Institute. Https://Www.Pmi.Org/Shop/P-/Elearning/Project-Management-Basics—-An-Official-Pmi-Online-Course/16125

PTSD: National Center for PTSD Home. (2021). *Traumatic Brain Injury And PTSD: Focus on Veterans*. Department of Veteran Affairs. Https://Www.Ptsd.Va.Gov/Professional/Treat/Cooccurring/Tbi_Ptsd_Vets.Asp

Purdue University. (2020, May 28). *Lean Six Sigma Online Certification & Training*. Purdue University. Https://Www.Purdue.Edu/Leansixsigmaonline/

Redbull. (2021). *Wingfinder: Red Bull Gives You Wings* - Redbull.Com. Https://Www.Redbull.Com/Int-En/Wingfinder

Rehabilitation and Prosthetic Services Home. (2021). *Blind Rehabilitation Centers and Locations*. VA.Gov | Veterans Affairs. Https://Www.Rehab.Va.Gov/PROSTHETICS/Blindrehab/Locations.Asp

Roto-Rooter. (2021). *Plumbing Apprenticeships*. Roto-Rooter Plumbing & Water Cleanup. Https://Www.Rotorooter.Com/Careers/Plumbing-Apprenticeships/

Samenow, S. (2018, July 10). *PTSD and crime: Another implausible causal linkage*. Psychology Today. https://www.psychologytoday.com/us/blog/inside-the-criminal-mind/201807/ptsd-and-crime-another-implausible-causal-linkage

SAMHSA. (2021). *Find Treatment*. SAMHSA - The Substance Abuse Mental Health Services Administration. Https://Www.Samhsa.Gov/Find-Treatment

Savino, C. S., & Krannich, R. L. (2010). *The Military-To-Civilian Transition Guide: A Career Transition Guide for Army, Navy, Air Force, Marine Corps & Coast Guard Personnel*. Impact Publications.

SHRM. (2021). *Military Eligibility*. SHRM - The Voice of All Things Work. Https://Www.Shrm.Org/Certification/Apply/Eligibility-Criteria/Pages/Military-Eligibility.Aspx

Stanton, D. (2020). *Free Career Training for Veterans - Certificates Included*. LinkedIn. Https://Www.Linkedin.Com/Pulse/Free-Training-Certificates-Veterans-Daniel-Stanton?Articleid=6677908287037444096

Stanton, D. (2021). *Free Career Training for Veterans - Certificates Included*. LinkedIn. Https://Www.Linkedin.Com/Pulse/Free-Training-Certificates-Veterans-Daniel-Stanton?Articleid=6677908287037444096

Student Veterans of America. (2021). *Inspiring Tomorrow's Leaders*. Https://Www.Studentveterans.Org

Technologies, B. (2021). *Air Force Skill Bridge Program*. Air Force Virtual Education Center. Https://Afvec.Us.Af.Mil/Afvec/Skillbridge/Welcome

Technologies, B. (N.D.). *Air Force's Premier Site for Information About Educational Benefits*. Air Force Virtual Education Center. Https://Afvec.Us.Af.Mil/Afvec/Public/Welcome

Texas A & M. (2021, March 26). *Veterans Benefits*. TEEX.ORG |. Https://Teex.Org/Program/Veterans-Benefits/

Transition Assistance Program. (2021). *Find Transition Assistance Program Classes Near You*. Transition Assistance Program. Https://Tapevents.Org/

Transition Assistance Program. (2021). *TAP Online Courses*. Https://Tapevents.Org/Courses

Tricare Online. (2021). *Tri-Care Online Medical*. Www.Tricareonline.Com. Www.Tricareonline.Com

Truity. (2021). *Understand Who You Truly Are*. Https://Www.Truity.Com

The University of Wisconsin. (2021). *Action Verb for Business majors*. Career & Internship Center | University of Washington. https://careers.uw.edu/wp-content/uploads/sites/25/2018/09/Action-Verbs-for-Resume-Writing-2016.pdf

UWM Career Development Center. (2021). *Action Verbs for Resumes*. The University of Wisconsin-Milwaukee. https://uwm.edu/careerplan/wp-content/uploads/sites/73/2014/01/Tipsheet-Action-Verbs-Tan-1.pdf

U.S. National Guard. (2021). *CREDENTIALING ASSISTANCE*. Army National Guard. Https://Www.Nationalguard.Com/Education-Programs/Credentialing-Assistance

United States Office of Personnel Management. (2016, August). *Pathways Programs Handbook*. OPM.Gov. Https://Www.Opm.Gov/Policy-Data-Oversight/Hiring-Information/Students-Recent-Graduates/Reference-Materials/Pathways-Programs-Handbook.Pdf

US AIR FORCE. (2020, May 6). *US Space Force: Air Force*. US SPACE FORCE. Https://Www.Spaceforce.Mil/

US Armed Forces Legal Assistance. (N.D.). *Search Legal Offices*. US Armed Forces/Air Force. Https://Legalassistance.Law.Af.Mil/

US ARMY. (2021, March 1). *Welcome to Army Credentialing Opportunities Online (COOL)*. Dod COOL Portal page. Https://Www.Cool.Osd.Mil/Army/

US Army. (2021). *It Starts with a Spark*. Armyignited. Https://Armyignited.Com

US Army. (2021). *Career Skills Program: SkillBridge*. U.S. Army Garrisons: U.S. Army Installation Management Command. Https://Home.Army.Mil/Imcom/Index.Php/Customers/Career-Skills-Program

USC Suzanne Dworak-Peck School of Social Work. (2017, September 26). *Service members speak out on difficulties of transitioning to civilian life*. USC Master of Social Work Blog. https://msw.usc.edu/mswusc-blog/transitioning-out-of-the-military

US Coast Guard. (2021, March 17). *Welcome to Coast Guard Credentialing Opportunities Online (COOL)*. DOD COOL Portal page. Https://Www.Cool.Osd.Mil/Uscg/Index.Htm

US Coast Guard. (2021). *Office of Work-Life Programs*. Deputy Commandant for Mission Support. Https://Www.Dcms.Uscg.Mil/Our-Organization/Assistant-Commandant-For-Human-Resources-CG-1/Health-Safety-And-Work-Life-CG-11/Office-Of-Work-Life-CG-111/Transition-Assistance-Program/TAP-Contact/

US Marine Corps. (2020, August 1). *Welcome to Marine Corps Credentialing Opportunities Online (COOL)*. DON COOL - Welcome to DON COOL. Https://Www.Cool.Navy.Mil/Usmc/Index.Htm

US National Labor Exchange. (2021). *Virtual Job Search Engine for the USNLX*. USNLX Virtual Jobs. Https://Virtualjobs.Usnlx.Com

US Navy. (2021). *Navy Fleet and Family Support Centers Locations*. FFSC - US NAVY. Www.Ffsp.Navy.Mil

US Navy. (2021). *Welcome to DON COOL*. Credentialing Opportunities Online/DON COOL. Https://Www.Cool. Navy.Mil/

USAA. (N.D.). *SCRA And Bank Benefits for Military Members*. Insurance, Banking, Investments & Retirement |. Https://Www.Usaa.Com/Inet/Wc/Bank-Military-Scra-Benefits

USO. (2021). *USO Transitions and Skillsoft Are Offering FREE Unlimited Access to An Entire Library of Training and Certification Tools*. United Service Organizations. Https://Www.Uso.Org/Skillsoft

VA Office Of Assistant Secretary for Information and Technology. (2021). *VA/Dod Ebenefits*. Department of Veterans Affairs, Https://Www.Ebenefits.Va.Gov/Ebenefits/Homepage

VA Public Health Home. (2021). *Exposure Related Health Concerns*. VA.Gov | Veterans Affairs. Https://Www. Publichealth.Va.Gov/Exposures/Health-Concerns.Asp

VA Staff. (2018). *VA-Benefits-Participant-Guide*. Department of Veterans Affairs. Https://Www.Benefits.Va.Gov/ TRANSITION/Docs/VA-Benefits-Participant-Guide.Pdf#

VA Staff. (2020, September 18). *Agent Orange Exposure and VA Disability Compensation*. Veterans Affairs. Https:// Www.Va.Gov/Disability/Eligibility/Hazardous-Materials-Exposure/Agent-Orange/

VA Staff. (2020, September 22). *Camp Lejeune Water Contamination Health Issues*. Veterans Affairs. Https:// Www.Va.Gov/Disability/Eligibility/Hazardous-Materials-Exposure/Camp-Lejeune-Water-Contamination/

VA Staff. (2020, April 30). *Choosing GI Bill Approved Schools*. Department of Veteran Affairs. Https://Www. Va.Gov/Education/Choosing-A-School/

VA Staff. (2020, November 12). *Disability Housing Grants for Veterans*. Veterans Affairs. Https://Www.Va.Gov/ Housing-Assistance/Disability-Housing-Grants/

VA Staff. (2020, September 22). *Exposure Through Project 112 Or Project SHAD*. Veterans Affairs. Https://Www. Va.Gov/Disability/Eligibility/Hazardous-Materials-Exposure/Project-112-Shad/

VA Staff. (2020, September 22). *Ionizing Radiation Exposure*. Veterans Affairs. Https://Www.Va.Gov/Disability/ Eligibility/Hazardous-Materials-Exposure/Ionizing-Radiation/

VA Staff. (2020, September 22). *Mustard Gas or Lewisite Exposure*. Veterans Affairs. Https://Www.Va.Gov/ Disability/Eligibility/Hazardous-Materials-Exposure/Mustard-Gas-Lewisite/

VA Staff. (2020, June 23). *VA Housing Assistance*. Veterans Affairs. Https://Www.Va.Gov/ Housing-Assistance/#Get-Va-Home-Loan-Benefits

VA Staff. (2020, September 22). *Veterans Asbestos Exposure*. Veterans Affairs. Https://Www.Va.Gov/Disability/ Eligibility/Hazardous-Materials-Exposure/Asbestos/

VA Staff. (2021). *Find A Yellow Ribbon School | Veterans Affairs*. Department of Veterans Affairs. Https://Www. Va.Gov/Education/Yellow-Ribbon-Participating-Schools/

VA Staff. (2021, January 4). *Gulf War Illnesses Linked to Afghanistan Service*. Veterans Affairs. Https://Www. Va.Gov/Disability/Eligibility/Hazardous-Materials-Exposure/Gulf-War-Illness-Afghanistan/

VA Staff. (2021, March 10). *How to File a VA Disability Claim*. Veterans Affairs. Https://Www.Va.Gov/Disability/How-To-File-Claim/

VA Staff. (2021, March 17). *Veterans Technology Education Courses*. Department of Veterans Affairs. Https://Www.Va.Gov/Education/About-Gi-Bill-Benefits/How-To-Use-Benefits/Vettec-High-Tech-Program/

VA Staff. (2021). *Serve Those Who Have Served Our Country*. VA Careers. Https://Www.Vacareers.Va.Gov/Careers/Transitioningmilitary/

VA Staff. (2021). *Pathway Program Requirements*. Department of Veterans Affairs. Https://Www.Va.Gov/EMPLOYEE/Pathways-Program-Requirements/

VA Web Solutions. (2021). *VA Locations*. VA.Gov Veterans Affairs. Https://Www.Va.Gov/Directory/Guide/Division.Asp?Dnum=3

Vet Center Program. (2021). *Vet Centers (Readjustment Counseling)*. VA.Gov | Veterans Affairs. Https://Www.Vetcenter.Va.Gov/

Veterans Health Administration,. (2021). *Public Health and Environmental Hazards, Office of Public Health, National Clinical Public Health Programs, HIV, Hepatitis, Public Health Pathogens Program*. HIV Home/VA. Https://Www.Hiv.Va.Gov/Index.Asp

Veterans4Quality. (2021). *About Veterans4quality*. Https://Veterans4quality.Org/

Vets2PM. (2020, November 21). *Blog »CAREER*. Https://Vets2pm.Com/Blog/

Wells Fargo. (N.D.). *SCRA Commitments –*. Wells Fargo – Banking, Credit Cards, Loans, Mortgages & More. Https://Www.Wellsfargo.Com/Military/Scra-Commitments/